THE STREAM

THE
STREAM

Robert Murphy

Pictures by Bob Hines

FARRAR, STRAUS AND GIROUX · NEW YORK

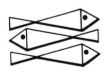

For Jean

There is a place much like this place,
but the people here are imaginary.

Tarry delight, so seldom met,
So swift to vanish,
Tarry still . . .

A. E. HOUSMAN

THE STREAM

THE TWO-THOUSAND-ACRE TRACT in the Pocono Mountains seemed not to belong to the raucous mid-twentieth century but to an earlier time, wooded, undisturbed, and untouched by the clutter of motels, summer cottages, "honeymoon chalets," golf courses, ski lifts, and their accompanying paraphernalia that proliferated around it; the four miles of stream that ran through it was sparkling and clean.

The ten men who had bought the tract around the beginning of the century had formed a club and held it to the original number of members. They had never exploited the land and, aside from building an access road partway along the stream, a single unobtrusive bridge, and a few rock dams, they had let it alone. They fished the stream and some of them hunted in the fall; they camped occasionally but built no houses. They lived and worked a hundred miles or so away in the crowded cities of the Eastern seaboard and wanted, so far as they could get it within reach, a little piece of wilderness for their recreation and retreat. The stream, named Fishkill by some long-forgotten Dutch pioneer (for the Dutch called streams "kills"), emptied into the befouled Delaware River near the village six miles below their property line.

The country in the tract, being the moraine of an ancient glaciation, was as full of rocks as the stream. Once it had been covered with magnificent trees so spaced that an oxcart could have been driven between them, for their high primitive canopy shaded out the growth of the forest floor. But the entire country had been clean-lumbered before the tract was bought, and only a few of the great oaks, beeches, hemlocks, and white pines remained among the second-growth forest that held it now. A few chestnut trees that had been too difficult for the lumbermen to reach had been killed soon after by the blight from China and stood dead and gaunt and gray on the hills.

The stream at its widest point didn't span much over seventy feet, and in these places it was shallow enough, except in the high water of spring, for a fisherman in waders to cross if he was careful of his balance and his footing. The bottom was rocky and there was a slippery coating of algae on the rocks; the fall of the land was sufficient to give the stream a rapid flow. A good deal of it was in white water and rapids; there were several low waterfalls where ledges of hard granite crossed it, and deep pools behind the rock dams.

It was a varied stream and no two reaches of it looked alike; any vista between the trees was beautiful, with gray rocks and green moss on the banks and sun glancing on the water. In the narrow

4

valley through which it had cut its way it wound between high, lichened rock ledges, between little flood plains holding small mossy swamps or past the mouths of other little valleys opening into it. Down some of these little valleys came small clear runs from higher springs.

The wood buffalo, larger and darker than their cousins of the Western Plains, the mountain lion and the wolf, and many other creatures which had once lived there had gone; so had the great flocks of passenger pigeons and the eagles which had once over-flown it. But there were many other animals left. The wonderful vitality that struggles to maintain the natural world against the multiplying encroachments of men, who were stupidly hostile or careless or anxious to exploit the land for what they could get out of it, upheld them; within this little enclave they made a stand against a contracting circle of neon lights.

There were thirteen major rock dams now along the length of the stream and big pools behind them, two low waterfalls, and four spring runs draining into the stream. Three of these runs wound through small swamps that were dark with hemlocks and spongy with moss; laurel grew in them, and marsh marigolds opened golden blossoms in the spring. Not far above the first pool, the clos-est to the highway, the stream was split by a rocky island; the bridge was above the second pool and the road ran to the eighth, crossing where it did because the land was flatter on that side. The small pools were unnamed; eight of the large ones had only num-bers and the others had been given names.

First Pool was below the lower falls; Bridge Pool was just below the bridge; S Pool, the ninth one, was named for its shape. The tenth pool was called Hemlock because a dozen or so great hemlocks leaned over it and shared the rock ledge that rose beside it with a thick growth of laurel and rhododendron, and Upper Falls Pool was just below the upper falls where a pair of horned owls had their nest. The spring run, which came into the stream between Third and Fourth Pools, above the bridge, ran through a swamp that was called Bear Swamp because at one time many years gone a big bear had been shot there. The other swamps and spring runs had never been named. One of the spring runs entered the stream between Fifth and Sixth Pools; one came in just above Hemlock; and the other, which was short and trickled with many small waterfalls down the precipitous slope of a stony hillside and over a mossy rock ledge, came in between Thirteenth Pool and the north boundary of the tract.

The stream ran roughly north to south, with many small changes of direction and windings, and was timbered along its entire length; shaded from the summer sun except for a few hours at midday, it was, even in the warmest weather, dappled with shadow and cool. In the spring, before the oaks and other deciduous trees along its course leafed out, it received sunshine that warmed the water sufficiently to bring out the early-hatching insects which had spent their larval or nymphal life beneath its surface.

This life was of an astonishing variety and complexity, a separate world from the one which began where land and water met. It began with microscopic life, a borderline world whose inhabitants were plants with some of the attributes of animals, and bacteria. Their functions were different. The plants, called phytoplankton, were the algae, desmids, and diatoms; they lived in the silt of the bottom, on the stalks of aquatic plants, adhered to the rocks, or drifted about in the quieter water. They were like the vegetation

6

ashore, harnessing the energy of the sun by photosynthesis to produce organic materials from the carbon, nitrogen, phosphorus, and other minerals dissolved in the water. The tiny fish and nymphal forms of insects that fed upon them, like the herbivores of the land, converted them to meat, which in turn was eaten by the larger fish and larger, predatory nymphs. Their waste products and the dead bodies of all were broken down and freed again for further use by bacterial decay.

The nymphal insects, hatched from eggs deposited in the stream by the flying insects that conceived them, took strange and diverse forms and grazed on the phytoplankton or caught the grazers and ate them; their forms depended upon the stream conditions that suited them. Some species of May-fly nymphs were rather rounded and burrowed into the bottom litter of calmer water to escape the current; some were flattened and had grappling claws and clung to rocks or hid under them in the current and moved freely about. The nymphs of the black flies, which sucked the blood of fishermen, glued themselves to rocks in the current and spun minuscule nets to catch the phytoplankton; caddis-fly nymphs made cases of tiny sticks or grains of sand in which they lived and crawled about on the bottom; dragonfly nymphs, with toothed lower jaws they could thrust out to catch other nymphs, moved about by expelling jets of water, and net-veined midge larvae possessed six suckers on their undersides so powerful that they could move across rocks in the swiftest currents and forage undisturbed.

These, then, were a few of the multitude of the stream's creatures; they were scattered about in riffles, in rapids and backwaters, in mosses clinging to the rocks, or in the silt and litter of the bottom according to their inclinations and the structures which had been developed over a vast span of time to enable them to fill the various niches of their environment.

They all comprised a great and complicated net of life in which each strand depended upon the others; anything that disturbed one egment of this life disturbed it all.

SPRING

O N E

THERE HAD BEEN many snowstorms during the winter, and as
the weather had been cold, the snow had accumulated and stayed
on the ground. It lay deep in the hollows and swirled in drifts
around the bases of the trees; no sooner had the wind blown it from
the hemlocks than a new storm laid another blanket of white upon
them, bowing down their branches. In the laurel thickets the leaves,
those indicators of temperature, stayed tightly rolled, and the shadows of the bare trees lay in a complicated cloud-blue tracery over
the soft contours of the snow where tracks of squirrels and other
creatures were soon blown over. Silence held a world that was
largely in monochrome except for the brief and cloudy flare of sun-
rises and sunsets; the silence of the nights was sometimes broken by
the hollow, ventriloquial booming of the pair of horned owls

nested in a tall pine near the upper waterfall, when the hunting bird and its mate sitting on the eggs called to one another. Horned owls nest very early in the year, for their young require a long time to feather and get on the wing; if the eggs had been left uncovered for very long, they would have frozen.

The stream was covered with ice for a good deal of its course and snow lay on the ice, concealing the water beneath; only here and there was it visible, swift and dark against the surrounding blanket of white. It had dropped a little since the first hard freeze, and there was an air space between it and the ice and behind the glittering icy columns that faced the waterfalls; in its turbulence it could still dissolve enough oxygen to sustain the multitudinous life of the stream.

In this cold and difficult season the metabolism of the water creatures slowed down, and on land insects and many animals slept the time away, but blue jays, juncos, and chickadees roamed the woods, ruffed grouse pitched into snowbanks for warmth on the coldest nights and found sustenance by eating buds, and the deer gathered together and yarded up in the thick hemlocks near Bear Swamp, trampling down pathways in the snow and eating what they could reach. The old female porcupine, who in softer seasons lived in a shallow cave in a rock ledge near Bear Swamp Run, took to an arboreal life; she had mated in October and, pregnant with her single young, spent the winter high above the ground, slowly climbing about and living off the inner bark of trees.

The winter had been long and hard, but its time was running out; finally the earth was swinging on its axis toward spring. At first the change was difficult to see, even if there was a different feeling in the air and an almost imperceptible difference in the sunlight as its angle changed, but the iron cold was tempered. The snow crystals began to melt and compact, and during the warmest part of the days tiny rivulets crawled beneath it toward lower ground. This happened slowly at first, with setbacks when the temperature fell, but little by little the tops of the tallest rocks came into view and the snow descended their sides. Snow fell from the hemlocks and the branches of the deciduous trees; and the underbrush, shaking off the weight of snow that had forced it down, swung slowly up again.

In the stream the ice thinned and broke and was carried clattering away, here and there piling up against the rocks and scraping off some of the diatoms, nymphal cases of insects, and the less securely anchored water plants that had clung to them. The stream was open now, and rising; in the forest surrounding it the buds began to swell and the yarded deer, hungry and thin, having eaten everything within reach of their pathways, began to move out and return to their old territories again.

The access road was still too deeply drifted for cars to use the afternoon that Jerry Ohlmstead, the only member who lived nearby, drove up the highway to the gate to see whether he could get into the tract. He and his wife had been good and affectionate companions until her death the year before, and she had shared his great affection for the place; they had fished together and she had walked the autumn woods with him when he hunted grouse or woodcock. He had been fifty-two years old when she died, and without her, in his new loneliness, he wanted to be near the tract and had sold his business in Philadelphia, bought a house in the village, and found a woman who lived there to do part-time housekeeping for him. Being alone now except for a distant cousin or two whom he seldom saw (for he had no other kin and the marriage had been childless), he was more than ever attached to the tract. This was only in a small measure sentimentality, for he wasn't a sentimental man; he had loved the outdoors since boyhood and spent all the time he could in it, and of all the places he had been and known he found this place the best. He had always been the most insistent about keeping the tract unchanged; it was still remembered about him that he had managed, seven years in the past, to squash a motion by two members whose wives had wanted an outhouse hidden in the woods.

He had missed wandering about in the tract and was impatient to begin again, but he saw that he would have to wait another week or two. He turned his engine off and sat in the car for a while looking into the woods he liked so well, a tall, rather lean, genial man with a good, snub-nosed, ruddy face whose close-cut dark hair was beginning to show a little gray. The shadows grew longer as the sun dropped toward the western ridge, taking on the cooler blue of approaching night, and Ohlmstead started his engine again and turned toward home.

The snowy owl, a large white bird spotted with black, having a fifty-five-inch wingspread and big yellow eyes, was a hunter of the Canadian tundra above tree line; swift and powerful, moving about by day as well as by night, it had lived upon the lemmings, rabbits, ptarmigan, and smaller game that it could catch. Ordinarily it lived well, moving south for a way in the winter as the other owls did, but the lemmings and rabbits that were its mainstay went through cycles of abundance and scarcity, and this year there had been a disastrous decline and a great deal of snow. Even in the owl's winter range it was almost impossible to find enough to eat, and, faced with starvation, it had drifted farther south with the other hawks and owls. Not many of them would return from such a migration, for they didn't know the country into which they would wander or the conditions that held in it, and there were many more people there. The snowy owl's size and color and habit of hunting by day made it highly visible, and every man's hand would be against it, for it would make a fine mounted trophy.

The owl had already covered a great deal of country and was forced to cover more. Besides the other owls there were goshawks from the great pine forests moving down, and the competition for scarce prey was extraordinarily keen. The owl was forced to seek a place that wasn't overhunted, and finally came to the upper reaches of the stream. No other predators from the north had happened upon the little valley, and the owl, hungry and thin, found game and stopped there.

Emaciated as it was, reduced to feeding on carrion when it could find it, the owl was fortunate that it had got so far. Even though it was wary of men on its lonely home range, it had in its desperation come too close to farms and small towns several times; it had been shot at twice and only poor marksmanship had saved it. The two men who had missed it would probably have rounded up their friends and searched for and killed it if there hadn't been so much snow in the countryside. Chancing upon a winter-killed deer scratched up and gnawed by the foxes in the Adirondacks had saved it before it reached the stream. Several weeks after that, it would have taken a porcupine and suffered a lingering death from the quills if the dangerous quarry hadn't scuttled just in the nick of time into a tangle of windfall timber too thick for attack.

For a time, while the owl built up its strength and its weight, it didn't move very far. Because of the deep snow the grouse spent a good deal of time in the trees eating buds, and the owl caught several of them; there was an occasional squirrel or rabbit, and one moonlight night it came upon two male skunks fighting, for it was their mating season, and took one of them and for a while was redolent of skunk. Mating time came for the raccoons, and they crawled out of their comfortable hollows where they were hibernating and moved about with such singleness of purpose that the owl managed to catch a young female. Fortunately its talons were driven deep into the raccoon's head and loin; if the talons hadn't been deep, the animal would have turned in its skin and badly injured its assailant.

Occasionally, when the wind was right, the owl heard the distant hollow booming of the horned owls farther down the stream, but the sounds meant little to it; there were no horned owls on the tundra, and it had never encountered these tigers of the night as large and powerful as itself. It didn't know they were nesting and would defend their territory with savage aggressiveness, and when its forays had diminished the possible prey nearby, it moved down the stream toward them.

The moon was full and the ice had gone from many parts of the stream. In the night the owl slid through the woods like a pale ghost and came to the upper waterfall. It hadn't seen any prey, and the big pool below the upper falls attracted it. It had often fished in its own territory during the summer, so it dropped to a low rocky shelf at the edge of the pool, lay down full length facing the water, and became still. All this took a very short time, and it was in readiness to thrust out a foot instantly at a fish or anything else that came near.

The female horned owl in the pine had been napping occasionally, but she was awake when the snowy owl dropped to the shelf; she caught the flutter of wings and the gleam of white in the moonlight. She had never seen a snowy owl, but its shape was unmistakable, and she knew it at once as an intruder that couldn't be tolerated. The owlets, which would hatch presently, would require an enormous amount of food, and there was no room in the territory for a big, hungry snowy owl.

The horned owl's eyes gleamed with cold fire and she got up off the eggs, walked to the edge of the nest, and launched herself in a swift and silent glide toward the other. The snowy owl's prone position and its turned back made it completely defenseless and the horned owl took advantage of it; she struck the other a stunning blow, taking it in the head and below the middle of the back. At the instant of striking, she opened her wings and beat the air, or they both would have gone into the water. The snowy owl, caught in the dreadful grip of eight talons, shrieked and leaped convulsively into the air, trying to get her own talons into the other; the moonlit woods, so silent a moment before, echoed with fiendish shrieks as they rolled and flopped wildly about, but the desperate struggles of the snowy owl were to no avail. Its assailant, eyes glaring and feathers erect, soon propped herself with her wings and drove her talons deeper; when the male owl, who had heard the uproar and made for it, came in, the snowy owl was dead. The female horned owl, panting and wild-eyed, was sitting on its corpse; presently she relaxed, shook her feathers into place, and the pair of them began to break into the dead owl and eat it. It had been fortunate and survived for a time, but now it would never again see its far-distant homeland or hunt the wide, open sweep of the tundra.

Well back from the stream on rising ground, in a shallow cave in a rock ledge that was concealed by hemlocks and a tangle of fallen trees, the black bear had given birth to her two cubs in January. Snow had drifted over the ledge and piled up before it; even in summer the cave was difficult to see and now, with the drift before it, it was invisible. Not many people had ever been that way in any event, for the area was covered with a great number and confusion of rocks that made walking very difficult and not worth the chance of a broken ankle to explore. Fishermen had no reason to climb that high above the stream, and deer and grouse hunters detoured around it. The bear had denned up there for the three previous years and had never been disturbed; shivering when the temperature dropped toward zero, with her breathing and circulation slowed down, torpid and lost to the world outside, she had avoided the difficulties of the hungry season.

She was four years old, had been on the tract for three of them, and these were her first cubs. Her mother had been shot at the upper edge of the tract when she was nearly half grown, and the experience had confirmed at an early age her instinctive fear of men and the old bear's teaching, for on several occasions when they had encountered man-scent the old bear had obviously been afraid of it and had cuffed the cub along before her as she fled from it. When she had fallen with a shattered heart the cub had been torn between confusion, great fear, and equally great yearning to stay with her

mother. She had run about, moaning in terror and indecision, moving to the old bear and away again, until the two men had run her off with sticks, stones, and shouts. The men were from the village where the stream joined the river; being a few yards inside the tract, they were poaching. It was illegal to shoot cubs, there was a little snow on the ground which would have showed their movements, and they didn't want to take the chance of shooting the cub and being caught with it and having on top of that a trespass charge laid against them. They would have shot had they thought they could get away with it.

It was probably due to this adventure, which increased her natural wariness, that the bear had reached her present age, for there was a good deal of hunting in the country. It wasn't hard to reach and there were quite a few men abroad in the hunting season; many of them had seen bear sign and every hunter in the village had finally heard about the cub and the opinion was that she was still about. The bear and deer seasons came at different times and there were many more deer hunters than bear hunters, but that she wasn't shot wasn't for lack of trying. So long as she stayed within the tract she had its protection, for the members were pleased to have a bear on the place and had agreed to let her alone. Like many hunted birds and animals in reach of sanctuary, she sensed in some mysterious way that she was safer in a certain area, and although a footloose bear may range for fifteen miles or so, she stayed within the tract or close to it.

When the cubs were born they weighed less than a pound apiece, blind, practically naked creatures about eight inches long, and their mother had awakened sufficiently to lick and fondle and nurse them and go to great lengths to keep them warm. Her sleep was not nearly so deep as it had been in other years, for between her love of them and their whimpering, squirming, and hungry demand for her milk, their rapid growth and increasing strength, she was forced to be more wakeful. She usually slept with her legs drawn under her, her head between her forepaws, lying over and covering them. The cubs grew rapidly. Their coats were first fuzzy and gray and gradually changed in shade to brownish black. Their eyes finally opened; they moved about more, and she slept and woke on the thick bed of leaves carried in the fall before.

There was still a good deal of snow lying about when she began to stir and get ready to come out of the cave. The stream was high and still rising, roaring between the banks, and every low spot in the woods held a little pool of water. Spring runs were full to overflowing; in damp spots the hardy hooked tips of skunk-cabbage blossoms were beginning to appear through the ground litter and fallen leaves of long-departed autumn, but little else was quite ready yet to seek the thin sunlight falling between the gray trunks of the trees.

The bear came fully awake slowly, stretching and grumbling to herself while the cubs whined and moved around her, finding her way through the fog that lay on her brain. When she had first gone into the cave she hadn't eaten anything for two weeks, she was very fat from constant feeding before that, and her belly and intestines had been empty. She had lived and nursed the cubs on her stored fat, the waste products of her lowered metabolism weren't excreted but increased in her blood and brought a sort of auto-intoxication to her; although conscious enough to care for the cubs, she was a little drunk, and had a drunken person's difficulty in waking fully. She did it fuzzily and with reluctance, but finally she got to her feet and walked uncertainly to the mouth of the cave. The cubs went with her, pushing around her feet and peering from beneath her at the world outside through the opening she pawed in the thin curtain of snow that still lay before the cave's mouth.

It was a clear day and for a time she stood swaying slightly and blinking at the brightness and shook her head as though to clear it; she sniffed and took a deep breath and blew it out again. The cubs, bright-eyed and curious, a little fearful of the dazzling, unfamiliar, and suddenly expanded world outside, wanted to get into it but were uncertain. They made little advances and retreats, licked the snow and were startled because it was cold and turned to icy water in their mouths. They whimpered, puzzled, and one of them—braver than the other—moved out a little way toward the lip of the ledge. She brought it back with a gentle paw and shook herself, seeing the tree trunks, the lichened rocks, the windfall timber before her and the scattered patches of snow as though through a thin and shifting curtain of cobwebs, and sat down on the lip of the cave until it should all grow solid and clarify itself.

She was in good condition, almost as fat as when she had renounced the world, and her coat was shiny and full; aside from an expression that was almost one of amazed stupidity, the long hibernation seemed to have had no effect upon her. After she sat there for a time, looking about and sniffing the scents of the outside world, she got up and worked her way slowly off the ledge, through the windfall, and on down toward the stream. The cubs followed, falling over themselves on the uncertain footing, dropping into her big tracks in the snow patches and scrambling out; occasionally she stopped and waited for them. When she reached the edge of the stream she stopped and stared at it as though she had never seen it before; and pushing the cubs behind her, she began to drink. She drank until her forelegs grew tired of holding her up, rested for a time, and drank again. She did this twice more, with an eye on the cubs, until her belly was distended and she was satisfied, and started off through the trees. She wasn't hungry and made no attempt to eat; she wouldn't eat for several days, until exercise and vast quantities of water would dissipate her hangover and bring her back to herself.

Having no destination and no desire for food, she wandered down the stream for a way, often waiting for the cubs or pausing to fill her marvelously acute nose with the scents of spring. Presently, in a little flat, she came upon a chipmunk standing on a stump. She stopped and the chipmunk, estimating that there was a safe distance between them, kept an eye on her but didn't retreat. It had come out of its burrow of many galleries to greet the spring, and intended to do it. Cocking its head at her, it flirted its tail and began to sing its little song of celebration: "Chock! Chock! Chock!" The almost birdlike notes grew a little louder and came closer together and soon reached other chipmunks on the edge of waking from their long sleep; first one appeared and then another until there were four of them. They skittered in closer to the first one and, mounting old anthills of stones, joined their voices to his in a chorus of welcome to the new season.

The cubs were startled by the chipmunks' singing and their quick movements; they crowded up to the old bear, whimpering and pawing at her, for they were hungry after their first walk as well as apprehensive. She sat down, swaying on her rump, and, taking a cub in each forepaw, held them to her breast to suck.

The happy energy that was in the chipmunks made their little striped bodies jerk and sway as they sang and forgot the possible perils that lay in wait for them; their song reached out and other chipmunks farther away woke to join them until, diminishing with distance, there were many of them within the bear's hearing. She sat pressing the cubs to her teats and listened to the chipmunks with a clownish expression that might have been pleasure.

Presently the chipmunks began to run about and greet each other, touching noses, pretending pursuits, and renewing old acquaintances, for they would soon mate. The cubs, having filled their little bellies, were ready to move again and explore the world that was so new to them; and because the chipmunks were dispersing, the old bear was also ready to go. She put the cubs down and the three of them marched away, angling off from the stream toward higher ground. Little by little the cubs began to deviate from their line behind the old bear, to take short side trips and sniff or paw at things that attracted their attention. Everything was new and they were full of curiosity, and as they got their legs under them and grew more accustomed to being out of the cave, they grew livelier. Occasionally, when they came together, they stood erect on their hind legs, sparred like boxers, and finally took hold of each other like wrestlers and rolled around on the ground. The old bear paused to watch these affrays, and if they seemed to her to become too rough she cuffed them apart with a heavy paw.

They wandered about, climbed to the top of the ridge where there was a lot of second-growth oak, and wandered down again; several deer moved off a way and watched them go by, and they crossed the porcupine's trail. The cubs were too interested in it; the old bear cuffed them away from it and led them in the other direction, whacking them a time or two to emphasize that they were to let porcupines alone.

The old bear had long since established a number of trails that she followed around the tract, as is the custom of bears, and this day she moved over many of them; she wasn't looking for food and probably wanted to see if there had been any changes during the winter. If there had been, she would have checked them out from several directions at a distance, but nothing appeared to disturb her and the day went by rather uneventfully; by late afternoon, when the sun was dropping low, they were all tired from their first day's wandering. They came to a rock ledge with an overhang where the ground was covered with leaves and free of snow, and she decided to sleep there. The cubs were hungry now and followed her under the overhang to be picked up and held to her breast, smacking their lips and grunting with satisfaction at the warm milk in their mouths. Presently, warm and full, they fell asleep; she put them down, caressed them with her nose, arranged herself to cover them, and dropped her head between her forepaws and fell asleep herself as the last light drained from the bare gray woods and the sky.

As they wandered through the succeeding days, the sun and the warming air that had brought them out began to wake a multitude of other small creatures beneath the fallen leaves or buried in the bottom of the stream. The little eastern tree frogs, "spring peepers," sang their tinkling chorus in the chilly nights; dormant toads and frogs and snakes began to stir, and insects or their eggs that had overwintered were coming to life. Mourning-cloak butterflies, which often appear before all the snow is gone, crept out of their winter hiding places and flew about in the woods. The first riotous run-off of water from the melting snow was over, the stream settled down somewhat, and the fishes' season of low metabolism and fasting was over; now they began to move about with increasing appetite, and lived to eat.

Ohlmstead was the only fisherman in the club who didn't fish exclusively with flies, which was a little odd of him, and he had as much difficulty as the rest of them with Upper Falls Pool, for the falls denied access to it from above, it was bounded on both sides by almost vertical rock ledges behind which the land rose steeply, and it was too deep to wade into from below. Old hemlocks hung over it, backcasts were almost impossible, and the currents and eddies that swirled about in it ruined the natural drift of a fly and the proper control of spinning gear. Beneath the surface the ledges were full of cracks and pockets and the bottom was a jumble of rocks; among the many good trout which lived in it was the largest one in the stream.

He was close to twenty-five inches long, deep-bellied and heavy, beautifully colored, a handsome old fish; having survived so long, he was very wary and suspicious and well able to take care of himself. He had long since explored the labyrinth of cracks and fissures that ran back in darkness under the ledges. Some of them weren't much wider than his body; some ran for many yards back under the earth and opened into each other, and they gave him a network of subterranean passageways into which he could retreat. Being the largest fish in the pool, he held the choice feeding station and chased lesser trout away from it. It was in front of a sunken rock where the current divided after dropping over the falls and eddies worked back, a dead spot where he could lie with little effort and see everything coming from above and decide whether to take it or not. From long experience he was a very selective feeder, and if anything aroused his suspicions he moved off into the recesses under the ledges and didn't emerge until after dark.

Ordinarily, like most big trout, he usually avoided his feeding station in full daylight and used it in early morning and late afternoon, but early spring always found him ranging more widely and in brighter light; he was very hungry after the winter's dearth and no fishermen had appeared as yet to alarm him. He fed all day, moving away from his station to root among the smaller rocks of the bottom to dislodge the nymphs or crawfish or snails that hid under them, dropping down to the riffles at the foot of the pool to see what he could find in the gravel there, and swimming up the spring run that came in below them. He didn't like the spring run, for it was shallow and clear, open to the sky for the lower half of its length, and empty of places to hide; but the rainbow trout which had been introduced into the stream were spawning there now, and he liked to eat their eggs.

The sky was overcast on the morning he first started for it, and between the narrow shafts of sunlight that occasionally broke through there were a few flakes of snow floating down. They melted as soon as they touched the ground and would presently stop falling, for it was late for snow. At his station the trout had snapped up a young mouse that had fallen into the stream and washed down to him, but there weren't many insects on the wing yet and nothing else appeared. He swung away from his station and moved along the bottom, catching an incautious crawfish that was backing out of a crack between two rocks, and picking up several caddis-fly larvae crawling about on the bottom in their cases of tiny sticks. The other trout he encountered moved out of his way; presently he was well down the pool and hung a foot below the surface for a time, floating up to inspect bits of debris on the surface and sinking again.

Before moving out into the riffles he hung in the tail of the pool for ten minutes to look about; the water was fairly deep there and the surface smooth, and his cone of vision was excellent. Over his head the surface was like a circular mirror, reflecting the bottom, but around it he could see full circle of the shore and the stream above and below him. The light rays from the surrounding world above the surface, entering a denser medium, were slowed down and bent at a sharper angle down through the water in the shape of a cone. His eyes were at the point, the apex, of this cone, which moved with him as he moved.

Not very far back from the stream, moving off in the direction of the spring run and the swamp, he saw the bears go by, the cubs bouncing about like black rubber balls; nothing else moved within his view to concern him. He slid over the lip of the pool and into the riffles, which barely covered his back. A pair of rainbows were spawning there, in a quieter little stretch of water that ran over pebbles behind a stone. He had come at just the right time for himself if not for them, for the female was releasing her eggs and the male was beside her releasing his milt over them; they were so engrossed in their mating that he was able to drift in behind them and swallow the eggs that didn't immediately sink to the bottom. By the time the female was finished, he had eaten a good share of the eggs and, drifting back a few feet, turned and swam to the spring run.

The run entered the stream beneath a canopy of rhododendrons with swelling buds, a clear run not over three feet wide and two feet deep, with mossy banks, shadowed by hemlocks and oaks coming into leaf, bordered by wild iris and other water-loving plants. With its bottom of fine gravel, cold and well aerated by tiny waterfalls, it was good spawning water, a fine nursery for young newts and newly hatched fish until they moved into the stream; the trout had mated there in the fall, and rainbows and suckers spawned there in the spring. The trout turned into it, not noticing the man standing motionless in his neutral-colored clothes beside a tree.

The man was Jerry Ohlmstead. He had come to the tract several hours ago, a few days before the trout season opened, to look around and walk the stream now that the snow was gone. Standing where he stood now, looking around and with plenty of time on his hands, he had been on the right side of the wind and had seen the old bear and the cubs go by in the distance and waited quietly to see what else might appear.

Wary as the trout was, it missed seeing the man standing so quietly and half concealed; Ohlmstead on his part was so startled by its size that he stepped out from behind the tree. The trout caught the motion and reacted at once; it whirled about and fled back toward the pool and into a crack in the ledge. In its swift retreat through the shallow riffles it raised an arrowing hillock in the water, and by jumping up on a stone Ohlmstead was able to follow its course. Because it had gone toward the pool instead of downstream, Ohlmstead knew that it lived there; it was the largest fish he had seen or ever heard about in the stream, and he immediately determined to catch it. He was well aware of the difficulties that the pool presented and knew how wary and experienced the fish must be to have grown so large, but these things only made the taking of it more attractive to him. He was excited by the prospect and well

pleased with his day. Not only was he back on the tract, which he held in great affection, but he had watched the bear (which no other member had ever seen) and he had located the best trout in the stream as well.

T W O

Here and there along the banks and scattered thinly through the gray trees the shadbush blossomed, opening delicate drifts of white flowers; in damp places the many small flowers of the red maples brought their brilliant color into the woods. To the casual eye the ground still seemed bare, a brown carpet of last autumn's leaves, but it was not bare. The first spikes of innumerable plants and bushes were coming through it, and scattered in sunny spots, close to the ground among the rocks and patches of moss, spring beauties, hepaticas and bluets and fringed milkwort, looking with its two purple wings and crested petal like a bird in flight, followed one another closely. Skunk-cabbage blossoms were fully emerged and the lovely small flowers of the trailing arbutus would soon be out in secret places difficult to find. The folded, domelike first leaves of May apples were pushing up, and starry bloodroot blossoms were opening; the fiddleheads of ferns were unfolding. They would overshadow the first small flowers seemingly too delicate and fragile to stand against the rough caprices of the early season.

Hidden in the warming earth, beneath the surface leaves, life had waked again as it had in the warming stream. Uncountable millions of creatures and the saprophytes which lived upon their bodies when life was finished with them were stirring to release the nutrients stored in the decomposing humus: bacteria, molds, fungi, mites, insect larvae, ants, centipedes, spiders, and worms; every rotting log housed its community of fungi, ants, beetles, millipeds, centipedes, and snails. Wood-boring long-horned beetles were at their work beneath the bark of trees, and spiders and hunting wasps began their search for prey. The queens of the bald-faced hornets and yellow jackets, which had been fertilized at the end of the previous summer and gone into hibernation, emerged, hunted suitable places to found new colonies, and began to lay eggs. Young cicadas which had spent up to seventeen years underground as nymphs were preparing to dig their way out and assume their adult forms, and the female king hornets that would catch them, in their larval forms in burrows, were pupating to dig their way to the surface, transform to adults, and hunt the new generation's cicadas to paralyze and lay their eggs upon. Young bumblebee queens were stirring in the abandoned meadow-mouse nests that had sheltered them, and newts that had hidden from the snow below the ground litter came to the surface to begin their pilgrimage anew.

All these and a vast multitude of others were awakening to the sun, and from a small, deep, winding cave in a ledge near the quaking bog on the ridge west of the stream the bats which had wintered wrapped in their wings would presently flit out. To find their path through the long tortuous dark labyrinth would be no problem for them, for they flew and hunted by the echoes returned to them when their ultrasonic squeaks (over a hundred thousand vibrations above what the human ear could catch) rebounded from any object before them; their small brains held an echo-memory of the way.

Almost as soon as the ground was free of frost, before most of the other migrating birds had reached the tract, the male woodcock flying north in stages by night from the edge of a marsh in South Carolina had swung away from the river and up the stream. It was his fourth long and dangerous journey, for he had been hatched on the tract three springs before; on his first flight south he had found stopping places along the way and had used them ever since. Like all his race he was a solitary traveler, sufficient unto himself, pausing here and there for a day or two to eat and rest. Because most woodcock migrate at about the same time, he had often encountered others in the covers where he stopped, but they had little to do with each other; mysterious birds, they were numerous in the covers one day and gone the next, and no man knew exactly when to expect them or how long they would stay.

The woodcock flew up the stream as the first pale edge of dawn was in the sky, over lower falls and the island, over the bridge and the next three pools, and turned in at the spring run that came in between Fifth and Sixth Pools. A screech owl which had had an unsuccessful night was sitting puffed up and morose on a dead branch of a hemlock there; it saw him and, jumping off the branch, dove to snatch him out of the air. His big dark eyes, as efficient in the darkness as any owl's, caught the movement and he reacted at once. He took a swift and abrupt turn into the hemlocks ashore, dodged through their branches like a bat, and still in swift twisting flight rose through them to lose the owl and leave it behind. He kept on, high, for several hundred yards, came to a tangle of young hemlocks, oaks, and briars near the spring, and dropped abruptly through them to the ground. He was home again; in this tangle, thick enough to be impervious to attack from the air and high enough above the spring and the little swamp to be dry, he had spent many of his days during the late summer and early fall of the previous year. He rested for a time and then, being hungry, moved out to the edge of the swamp to probe the soft ground with his long bill for worms.

He was a strange little bird, much studied by men but still not very well known, secretive, a lover of the twilight and the dark. His bill had a sensitive and flexible tip to find worms and take hold of them underground; his ears, the better to hear their faint stirrings in the earth, were on the lower side of his head instead of higher and behind the eyes as in most birds, and his eyes were placed near the top of his head to show him instantly the way upward through the thickets if some predator surprised him as he probed the ground.

He found a few worms and went back to the tangle again to sleep until twilight, so beautifully camouflaged with soft blacks and grays, russets and browns, that he was all but invisible and lost among the shadows and the fallen leaves.

For several days the woodcock fed close to his resting thicket, and then began to range more widely to find other feeding places, flitting about like a little dark ghost in the half light. Once he saw the bear and her cubs in the swamp near the upper falls, the cubs bouncing about and sparring with each other in a final bout before settling down for the night; the old dog fox that lived off the tract but often ranged about in it stalked him twice without success.

Soon he began to grow restless and one evening just before sundown flew north a quarter of a mile to the top of the ridge where there was a clearing. It was his singing ground; he had mated there the previous year. He came down in the middle of it and after standing still for a short time began to strut around with his tail spread, his bill resting on his chest, uttering a metallic, rasping, nasal "Peent! Peent!" These sounds, which carried for a surprising distance, were alternated with soft, guttural notes. Suddenly he jumped into the air and rose in a spiral, continuously twittering, until he was several hundred feet in the air. At the top of his pitch he began a series of four musical, descending notes, sweet, beautiful, and clear, and continued them as he zigzagged swiftly and erratically down. They ceased as he neared the ground; he landed and began the peenting call again as he strutted around.

He continued to alternate the singing flights and the calls from the ground until the afterglow faded from the sky. They were his love song to attract and impress a mate, extraordinary in a bird usually so silent and fond of seclusion.

He returned at dawn and made his singing flights and peenting calls until full daylight, but no female woodcock appeared; she didn't come until the following evening during the afterglow. Singing, he tumbled recklessly down and approached her full of

ardor, but she didn't want to be hurried. They began to play, running around each other in a little circle, their heads back and their long bills pointing upward, their wings lifted and their feathers puffed out, in a sort of dance that was absurd and touching. Then the male jumped into the air again, to woo her with more song.

Not far away, Ohlmstead, who had been there on the two previous evenings, stood quietly watching and listening, filled with delight. He had long thought that there must be a singing ground on the tract and had found it the preceding year. Woodcock and grouse, which many hunters think our finest game birds, were favorites of his, and of the two the woodcock, mysterious little haunter of the twilight, traveler over half the continent by night, stirred his imagination more. The drumming thunder of a mating grouse in the spring woods was a splendid thing, but this love song of the small troubador, lyrical and sweet as it descended from the evening sky, moved him more deeply; he had first heard it years ago in Nova Scotia, on the first trip he and his bride had made together. It had brought them even closer to one another, for they had discovered then that they shared a desire to enter into the hidden and mysterious lives of the creatures about them.

The singer plunged down again and vanished into the shadows; presently Ohlmstead turned away and walked through the darkening woods to his car.

Waves of warblers, small, shy, and elusive, some of them staying high in the trees and others flitting through the underbrush or the evergreens, appeared from their winter homes in the south and passed through on their way to northern nesting grounds. Most of them migrated at night; many of the males were brightly colored in their mating plumage, but in their rather secretive comings and goings through the day they were less noticeable than the bright, noisy jays who lived on the tract or the white-breasted nuthatches who had spent the winter there and would soon go north. Some of the travelers—catbirds, veeries, red-eyed vireos, yellow-breasted chats, scarlet tanagers, yellow-throated and blue-throated green warblers, wood thrushes, kinglets, and wrens—had nested here before and now were home again, and newcomers found the little valley to their liking; the woods became more lively with their songs and their flittings, their territorial squabbles and their mating and nesting. A pair of big, pileated woodpeckers, black and white, the male with a fine red crest, appeared on the stream and began to chisel out a nesting hollow in a tree above S Pool, drumming loudly and slowly, giving their ringing calls, and showy in their bold colors about the stream. A pair of broad-winged hawks dropped out of a migrating company of their fellows where the stream met the river, and returned to their old territory near the swamp that emptied into the stream between Hemlock and Upper Falls Pools. An old male kingfisher, driven a little farther south when ice and snow had hidden the water, came back and was presently joined by a mate; flashes of blue, they flew with their rattling calls up and down the stream. The ancient Greeks had called them *halcyons,* quieters of rough winds and bringers of fair weather while their eggs were hatching.

The six crows that nested and spent their easier seasons in the tract but had gone several hundred miles south for the winter and roosted at night along the river with thousands of their fellows returned and began their courtships, becoming sly and secretive. They had no time now for their usual investigations of everything about them and their rowdy comments upon it. Soon after they had paired, the horned owls, whose young had hatched, picked off two of them from different pairs on succeeding nights, causing confusion and quarreling among them. The survivors of the two pairs were both males and, after bedeviling the mated pair and unsuccessfully trying to break them up, drifted off to search elsewhere for mates. The other birds on the tract would never realize how many of their eggs the owls—which were otherwise a constant threat to them—had saved.

Two-thirds of the way between the stream and the spring at the head of Bear Swamp Run, well back from the run and several hundred feet above it on the hillside, there was an old beech tree with a big hollow limb; it was in this hollow that the pair of raccoons had spent the winter, sleeping the difficult season away, curled up together and warm. Spring had brought them out and for a time they had wandered about together, hungry and thin, trying to find enough to eat, sprawling on the limb in the warmest part of the day to take advantage of the sun. On the night of the full moon the female had returned to the hollow by herself, and when the male returned later she wouldn't let him in. Her four young, her first ones, were about to be born, and she didn't intend to trust him near them for a few days: she met him at the hollow's entrance with growls and a show of teeth. This was most unusual behavior on her part and he churred and complained and tried to touch noses with her to show his fine intentions, but she would have none of it; finally, puzzled and rebuffed, he gave up and descended the tree.

It was nearly dawn, and he needed a place to sleep. A little at a loss after his sudden eviction, he wandered down to the spring run, making a soft, complaining churring to himself. Near its end the run went through a culvert under the road and entered the stream through the rhododendron thicket, close to the place where Ohlmstead had been standing when he saw the bears and the trout, and the raccoon went through the culvert and the thicket and paused at the edge of the stream. It slid past him, steely gray in the wan light with a little mist trailing over its surface, and while he stood there a pregnant doe came quietly to the edge of Third Pool a little below him, on the opposite shore, to drink. She approached the water daintily, with several pauses to look about, her head up and her ears cocked, drank, and went back into the timber again. She lived above the stream on higher ground, to the west, on the edge of a clearing now growing up with brush and young oaks and hemlocks, and would have her fawn there; it would be a little time yet.

The raccoon, always curious and interested in the life around him, watched her until she had disappeared and then went back to the road, crossed it, and started up the other side of the spring run. He had remembered an old broad-winged hawk's nest in a beech that he and the female had found in their climbing about the fall before, and made for it. Among the most curious of animals, always ready to investigate everything he came across, he didn't hesitate now. The light was growing stronger; squirrels and chipmunks were out, and the birds were beginning their morning choruses. One of the crows drifted over, caught sight of him, and circled to caw its disapproval; this brought up a catbird that followed for a way and scolded at him. He quickened his pace, got to the beech, climbed to the crotch where the old nest was, and settled himself for the day.

That evening, after surveying the world from the old nest, he crossed the spring run on an old log and went first to the den tree. His mate had heard him climbing the trunk, met him at the opening of the hollow, and sent him off. He went down the tree head-first, like a squirrel, his hind feet reversed for brakes, and set out on his evening explorations.

The peepers were trilling in the swamp along the run, but he wasn't much interested in them; their small size and their perches in the brush made them too difficult to catch and not worth the catching. He moved slowly on until a larger green frog jumped up ahead of him and dove into a weedy little puddle in the moss and hid itself. Even in daylight the eye wouldn't have been able to discover it, and he didn't try to find it by sight; he waded into the puddle, settled his weight on his hind legs, and staring blankly off into space began a delicate exploration with his forepaws that were so much like human hands. One of them finally touched the frog and before it could jump again both of them closed on it. He killed it with a bite, sloshed it up and down in the water to wash off the mud, and ate it.

As he was finishing it a pair of barred owls which always nested a little off the tract landed with ghostly silence in a tree not far away and after an interval of ludicrous bowing and nodding to each other cooed softly several times and then began to hoot, chuckle, and laugh like madmen at the full power of their lungs. The uproar they made was spectacular, filling the woods with wild and vehement sounds like those supposedly made by maniacs or demons, the shrieking, rhythmic Wha! Wha! and Hoo! Hoo! Hoo! interspersed with tender coos and chuckles, laughs, and hollow reverberating growls. They had the name of being the noisiest of owls and lived up to it, yelling at one another, bowing with half-opened wings, and wobbling about on the limbs where they sat; for sheer carrying power and versatility of weird clamor, their courtship was probably the most extraordinary in the animal kingdom.

When they began, the raccoon paused and stared upward at them; as they went on he moved off, shaking his head to clear it. Their hullabaloo followed him as he made his way down the run, and they took off to fly farther up the stream and start anew. The horned owls answered them and the woods rang with a bloodcurdling uproar which was now softened by distance, and the raccoon went through the culvert and ambled along the stream to Third Pool, where he waded in and worked his way slowly around the pool's edge, squatting and feeling under the stones. He caught several crawfish and presently another frog, and left the pool to cross the road again between the culvert and the bridge below. There was a thicket there bordering the Bear Swamp and as he quartered about in it the scent of a veery came to him. It was nested a few feet off the ground and the scent was fragmentary and faint but he worked around to locate the source of it, occasionally standing on his hind legs to get his nose higher in the air. Finally he had a rough fix on its position and, climbing into the thicket, swung about like a monkey until he came to the branch that held the nest. The sitting bird flushed off into the darkness; the branch was so thin that he couldn't walk out on it, but he hung dangling by his forepaws and worked his way out. The branch sagged, the eggs finally rolled out of the nest, and he dropped to the ground and ate them.

His belly was comfortably full now but his curiosity was as keen as ever. He left the thicket and ambled down the side of the road until he came to the bridge. The wind was from his back and gave him no indication that there was a man in Bridge Pool; because of the brush along the road, he didn't see the flashlight playing on the water until he was on the bridge itself. He stopped at once, his sharp little muzzle pointed at the mystery and his ears and eyes intent. The pool was open to the sky, and in the starlight he could make out the dark figure of the man standing almost to his hips in the water.

The man was a poacher and his name was Slattery; he lived outside the village in a shack in the woods back from the road which ran from the village past the tract. He had an excessive fondness for the bottle and never held a job long; when the notion moved him he walked through the woods to the stream and stole some fish. There would be more of them now than later, after the season opened and the members began to catch them, for though there was always a good hatch of young trout in the stream the club supplemented it with several hundred hatchery fish, and Slattery always took advantage of this windfall.

Tonight he had a frog gig on the end of a pole and with the help of the flashlight had already gigged several nice trout, but he decided that this wasn't productive enough. He came out onto the bank, where he had a friction-top can with powder and a fuse in it, lit the fuse, and tossed the can out toward the head of the pool. The explosion would stun the fish, which would float belly-up on the surface, and he would gather them up as the current brought them to the pool's foot.

The explosion came when the can was halfway down the pool, jarring the earth and sending the water flying. The raccoon jumped a foot off the ground, turned in the air, and galloped up the road the way he had come.

The cock ruffed grouse, a wary bird and an expert in the tricks that made his race admired by hunters who loved a difficult and unpredictable quarry, hadn't survived for four years on the tract by relaxing his constant vigilance and exposing himself. In one way or another he had circumvented the best efforts of hawks, owls, foxes, weasels, or men to get teeth or talons or a charge of shot into him; in those inevitable moments when his alertness had been betrayed by circumstances a turn of luck had saved him. Because the first two hunters who had fired at him had been bad shots he had lived long enough to learn to flush out of range, crouch until the man went by and then flush behind him, or quickly get a tree between himself and the hunter when he burst into the air. If the man had a dog, he didn't hide; he drifted ahead of it, and flushed far out of range. Men only shot at him for a month but his other enemies had to be avoided all the year around; it was only in the spring, when the mating urge took hold of him, that he became in any degree heedless of them.

He had been growing increasingly restless, and the morning came when his restlessness became specific. He had spent the night in a thick stand of hemlocks on the high ground west of S Pool, where he roosted all winter, and in the early dawn he took off, his wings clattering among the hemlock branches, and flew with reckless speed through the woods to land near a mossy old log in another hemlock thicket a hundred yards from the woodcock's daytime cover. The light was still dim in the thicket: even in the middle of the day a coppery gloom held it, and after walking up

and down the log the grouse opened his wings and made several almost silent strokes with them. Then he lowered his tail against the log, stood erect with his crest raised and his wings dropping and suddenly made a forward stroke with them that was too quick for the eye to follow, making a thump upon the air. The wings were drawn swiftly back and another stroke made, and another and another, a series of thumps accelerating to a throbbing blur of sound, hollow and ventriloquial and far-carrying through the spring woods, a sound made by no other bird.

His lowered tail had braced him against the powerful backward thrust of his wings, and when the drumming was over he raised it from the log and relaxed for a few minutes before beginning to drum again. With rests of five minutes or so between the drummings, he drummed for two hours; toward the end of that time a hen grouse, which had flown in from farther down the stream and landed at the edge of the thicket, stole into the gloom beneath the hemlocks and they saw each other at the same time. The hen stopped; the cock stared fixedly at her, spread and raised his tail into a fan, dropped his wings, and erected the black ruffs of his neck. He took several strutting steps along the log, hopped to the ground, and strutting toward the hen began to shake his head rapidly and hiss.

The hen was brought to acquiescence by this display and lowered herself submissively to the ground. The cock gave a long final hiss and ran toward her, quivering, but instead of mounting her began to buffet her savagely with his wings and knock her about. She was dazed for a moment by this attack, and then escaped from him and fled.

The cock flew back to the log, shook himself, walked back and forth, and then began to drum again. He was full of hostility; in several more days he wouldn't attack the hens that came to him, but in this early phase of his mating cycle he seemed unable to recognize the sex of other grouse and was ready to fall upon all comers viciously to drive them out of his territory.

THREE

As though to make up for the severity of the winter, spring had come on very rapidly; leaves were unfolding more than usual when the trout season opened and fishermen appeared on the stream. Because there had been no one about for so long, the bear and her cubs had spent a good deal of their time near the stream and the spring runs, for they found more to eat there, but almost stumbling upon one fisherman and catching the scents of several more, the old bear moved out toward the boundaries of the tract. The cubs, which had grown considerably, didn't want to go. Moving water fascinated them, they loved to slop about in it and try to catch the things that lived in it, and there was more variegated life close to it than there was away from it. The wonderful net of scents or the frogs along the banks, the kingfishers—flashes of blue—rattling up and down the stream, the big pileated woodpeckers' sharp calls, a salamander or an old box turtle or anything else that moved or could be bedeviled added to their entertainment.

They climbed trees and were very slow in responding to her commands to come down, their games always seemed to take them back toward the stream, and they appeared to plan all their other movements with a sly return in mind; they were like bad little boys whose only object in life is to get into the forbidden jam closet. Bright-eyed, inquisitive, and full of bounce, their little bellies round and their black coats shiny from her milk and the roots she dug for them, they gave her no respite. Her temper grew shorter and her forepaws heavier; she cuffed them with increasing frequency, until it would seem that she would punish the life out of them, and they throve on it. Knocked head over heels, they squalled and bounced up again and set about earning another cuffing.

After the old bear had made up her mind to leave the stream, she only swung back toward it once, into the vicinity of Upper Falls Pool, for the wind had brought her the scent of a doe which had been killed running into a sharp branch that had torn open her jugular vein. She lay across the stream beyond Twelfth Pool, and following the scent the bears passed close to the tree where the horned owls had their nest. One of the cubs began to climb the tree and the female owl, which was sitting in a nearby hemlock with its feathers pulled in close to its body, its horns erect and its eyes closed to slits, heard the cub's claws and was wide awake at once. Its big yellow eyes glared, it puffed up its feathers, and snapping its beak with fury it spread its great wings, launched itself out of the hemlock, and struck the cub a blow on the back of his head with its talons that knocked him out of the tree. He fell, grabbing at

56

branches and caroming off them, turning somersaults, squalling with pain and fright, and hit the ground with a thump.

The old bear, roaring, rushed over to rescue him; the owl, hooting with rage, swooped past him, and the old bear rose on her hind legs and batted at it. The male owl came swooping like a shadow in through the branches and the pair of them flew about or perched nearby, snapping their beaks metallically and adding their angry, growling hoots to the uproar. Both cubs ran to their mother and tried to swarm up her legs and she cuffed them off the better to attend to the owls, turning quickly to follow their flight and ready to swing at them, but the owls stayed higher in the trees now and contented themselves with beak snapping and hooting.

The affair having come to a stand-off, there was a lull. The cub that had been struck was still whimpering and had a bloody head and wouldn't leave his mother; she licked his wounds, cuffed him, and decided to leave the field to the owls. With many pauses and backward looks to make sure they would stay where they were, she led the cubs off toward the stream. When she reached it and found that the enticing scent of the deer came from the other side, she turned up the stream to find a log to cross upon or a fallen tree that spanned it; the cubs, momentarily chastened, followed her in single file.

Ohlmstead never fished on weekends, when many of the other members were on the stream; he not only liked to have the water to himself but felt that their opportunities were limited while his were not and that it was only fair to give them as much elbow room as he could. He would have missed the survey crew's state truck pulled up beside the road on a weekend; when he saw it, as he was driving to the stream early on a Tuesday morning, he stopped behind it and got out of his station wagon. He was curious as to why it was there, for the tract's eastern boundary wasn't much farther along the road. The tree men hadn't, apparently, been there very long; they were standing at the rear of the truck and hadn't opened it yet.

"Morning," he said. "You're out of bed early."

They returned his greeting easily and the oldest of them, who seemed in charge of the crew, said: "You didn't sleep very late either. By the look of your jacket, you might be going fishing."

"I had it in mind," Ohlmstead said. "It keeps me young. The Lord doesn't count the days of a man's life that he spends fishing."

"That's good news," the older man said. "They owe me about three years, then. I did a lot of it when I was a kid. Where do you go?"

"I belong to the club up the road," Ohlmstead said.

"Oh," the man said, and the three of them looked at each other quickly and back to Ohlmstead again.

He caught the look and had a sudden little feeling, almost a premonition, of possible trouble or disturbance in the future, for he was particularly alert to anything that might encroach upon the tract even though he knew that it couldn't be held inviolate forever. "Are you changing the road, or shifting it?" he asked.

"No," the man said, after a short silence. "No, I haven't heard anything about that."

The man's hesitation made Ohlmstead think that he was concealing something, that he had been told not to talk; he thought of the devious ways of politicians, or secretive land deals for a profit, and the right of eminent domain used for the advantage of a few. His misgivings grew stronger. "What, then?" he asked. "Not that I want to stick my nose into your business, but I'm naturally interested in anything that might affect us."

"Sure," the man said. "I would be, too. You have a nice thing in there, and there aren't many like it left. A little more squeeze all the time, people having too many kids and overrunning everything. When I was a kid, now . . . But all I know is we're going to run a line about here—" and he gestured roughly north and south, at right angles to the highway—"pretty much along the top of the ridge. It won't be on your place, it'll be a little way from your boundary. I don't know what they want it for. Hell, I'm only an engineer."

Ohlmstead looked at him and felt that he was telling the truth, or at least as much of it as he was going to. He'd have to find out more, if he could, somewhere else. "Thank you," he said. "I'll be on my way and let you get to work." He raised a hand, they raised theirs in return, and he got into his car and drove to the gate of the tract.

He got out and unlocked it, drove the car through, locked it again, and went on. He always felt a little excitement as he entered the tract, as though each entrance would be a new adventure not experienced before, each turn of the road reveal a new pleasure or some hitherto unseen creature caught in an instant of surprise. The serene air of the place, like that of the river that some long-dead poet thought would go on in quiet beauty forever, was like balm to his spirit. Today he was somewhat preoccupied by the encounter he had just had; the pleasure was dimmed a little. The club had been very fortunate in being largely undisturbed for so many years, but what was called progress was catching up with them, and who could be lucky enough to avoid it forever? He suddenly wondered if this, perhaps, would be the year their luck would begin to run out, and then quickly told himself that this was nonsense, that it was ridiculous to begin hanging crepe just because he'd seen a survey crew. They were always tacking little pieces of rag to the roads, and besides nothing else had appeared to encourage such gloomy thoughts. He shook his head and drove on.

The road was high at first and away from the stream, through second-growth oak, but it dropped as it wound about and approached the little valley's floor. More hemlocks bordered it and more moss glowed green in the low, damp spots; the road reached the bridge, and on the bridge Ohlmstead stopped, as he always did. There were rocky rapids just below him and then Bridge Pool, wide and smooth; above him were Third and Fourth Pools between stretches of fast water before the stream turned, overhung with trees, the fast, clear water glinting where the sun touched it and gleaming white where it dropped over the dams.

It was a lovely view, enlivened by the hurrying water, unspoiled and seemingly untouched, with spring flowers scattered through the woods and new life everywhere either already born or about to be born. Ohlmstead thought again of the three men and then resolved to forget them for the rest of the day and drove on. The road wound about through the hemlocks and laurel and oaks and wild azalea, climbing a little, dropping a little, but along the stream now and in view of it most of the time, until it ended near Eighth Pool. Ohlmstead got out of his car, went around to the back, and decided to use his fly rod today; he set it up and before he had tied on the Cahill the black flies found him. They were hatching in myriads now, after their larval life in the stream. They were soon around his head in clouds, whining in his ears and blundering into his eyes, biting like tiny hot needles, the penalty of early-spring fishing. When the leaves opened more fully most of them would be higher in the trees, but now they were a tribulation. Before he pulled on his waders he smeared himself with repellant and lit a rank black cigar that would hold them off a little way.

With the cigar clamped in his teeth he picked his way through the brush and the lichened rocks to the head of the pool and stood for a moment just to enjoy being there.

A hunting wasp had stung and paralyzed a big black spider near his feet and, rather than try to fly with it, towed it across the surface toward a hole it had dug in the other bank. Watching it, Ohlmstead was reminded again of the three men, but shook his head and put the memory out of his mind. He wet his fly and cast it across the pool. It sank and drifted down with the current; as the line straightened out and the fly swung and rose toward the surface like a May-fly nymph coming off the bottom to emerge, a good fish took it with a rush. Ohlmstead raised the rod tip to set the hook and the line tightened and hissed through the water. The rod danced, and Ohlmstead, grinning with pleasure, puffed out a great cloud of smoke and played the fish.

About an hour and a half later, as he was happily fishing S Pool, he was startled by an airplane roaring overhead, flying low and trailing a dense pale cloud of spray. He had been vaguely conscious of hearing it farther away several times before but had been so concentrated on his fishing that he hadn't paid much attention; this time he couldn't ignore it, and ducked his head as the misty spray settled slowly about him.

Angered by the plane being there, by the fact that the state was scattering an insecticide over the tract without permission, whether the club wanted it or not, without even advising them that it would be done, he climbed out of the stream and sat down on a flat stone on the bank. He knew that there had been a local outbreak of fall cankerworm, a destructive caterpillar of the measuring-worm family which defoliated orchards and other deciduous trees, some miles to the west of them the previous year, but he hadn't seen any of them on the tract. It was apparent that someone, some bureaucrat or other, had arbitrarily decided that a larger area should be sprayed to contain this local outbreak. But didn't they, the owners of the tract, have the right to decide whether or not this dubious shotgun approach should be inflicted on them? Or even the right to discuss it before it was done?

He didn't like the insecticides they were using nowadays; he was afraid of them, for he had read Rachel Carson's *Silent Spring* as well as a number of articles on the subject and was aware of the rising tide of opinion that the chlorinated hydrocarbons should be used only under rigidly controlled conditions, if at all. Although his knowledge of them was general and rather fragmentary, picked up here and there, he had gathered that they were very long lasting and cumulative, affecting insect life beneath the surface of the ground and the water or above it, and the spawning of fish and the hatching of birds. This would have a bearing on the life of the tract for some time to come, but he didn't know how much. He decided to write to a research biologist he had gone to school with and see what he could find out.

The plane returned higher up the western ridge on its next transect, still emitting spray, and disappeared. He looked after it, frowning, and decided that the fun had gone out of fishing for the day. He was upset by the spraying, which was unnecessary and had come so soon after his unpleasant thoughts about the survey crew, and the glow of pleasure had left him.

He was downcast by the fact that a protest would accomplish nothing except possibly prevent a second spraying. He would have been more downcast had he known that a careless mistake had been made when the spray's ingredients had been mixed, and that it was stronger than it should have been. A single spraying with the standard formula would have been undesirable enough, particularly when it wasn't necessary, but human error had compounded its effect. The insects it killed wouldn't be the only victims; potent for years, it would lie in the soil and be leached into the stream, altering the balance of invertebrate life and affecting the lives of birds and fish that lived on the invertebrates and the lives of their young. Many would have survived a single spraying of the standard formula; now there would be fewer of them.

Ohlmstead was of course unaware of this, but he was sufficiently concerned to get off a note to Alec Goodenow, the club's president, when he got home. He wrote:

Dear Alec:
The tract was sprayed from the air today. Don't ask me why, for we've no infestation of anything. From what I've heard, this stuff is bad news, and I think it would be a good notion to write the state and protest, which might at least save us from a second or maybe even third shot and keep the concentration down. A state survey

crew has started work near our eastern boundary, but I couldn't find out why. Maybe you can. These two things in one day make me jumpy, I hope unnecessarily.

The fishing's been good. Try to come up.

Yours,
Jerry

SUMMER

ONE

THE DOE which lived near the old clearing on high ground to the west of Third Pool delivered her fawn before daybreak and after cleaning it thoroughly lay next to it to keep it warm. It was her first one, a little brownish-yellow white-spotted male creature weighing not quite four pounds; by the time the sun was up, it had staggered onto its shaky legs and nursed for the first time and then laid down again, curled up with its chin resting on the ground by its folded legs, and its ears laid back. With the rising sun dappling the ground around it, it was almost invisible; only its eyes moved as little by little it grew accustomed to its new world. An occasional bird fluttered nearby, ants and beetles crawled about, leaves moved in the light breeze; the fawn lay very still, instinctively avoiding calling attention to itself. The doe left it, moving off a few yards, looking all about, listening, and testing the air before bedding down.

Her home range wasn't very large; whitetails probably have a smaller range than any other American deer. The old clearing was brushy and growing up into woods again, but there was still enough sunlight in it and plenty of browse; along with the woods surrounding it, there was good cover. A quarter of a mile away, on top of the ridge, there was a quaking bog; long ago it had been a shallow little spring-fed pond; the sphagnum moss had extended out into it, supporting other water-loving plants, and covered it over. Beneath this blanket it was like a wet sponge, held away from the sun and air, cold and acid; Labrador-tea bushes shared it with pitcher plants, and it was a little community different from the slightly higher land that surrounded it. Blueberry bushes grew in profusion among the gray rocks around its edges, and a little farther back there were tamaracks; it was a little island seemingly brought from much farther north and set down on top of the ridge.

The doe could get water there, even if its taste was unpleasant, and would while the fawn was too small to travel, for it was closer than the stream. The nearest farm was a mile or so to the west, and when she was alone she sometimes joined other deer there by night to feed on the crops. Men seldom came into her range, but if they did she could skulk about, silent-footed, in an area that was thoroughly familiar to her, and avoid them. Few animals can make better use of cover than a whitetail deer.

She came to the fawn and fed it several times during the day and when the sun was setting moved off to the bog to drink. Concern for the fawn kept her moving at a good pace; she passed a grouse on its way to roost, and farther on, a weasel on the prowl bounded across the deer trail twenty yards in front of her. As she drank from a little pool at the edge of the bog, one of the horned owls went over her in its soft-feathered, silent flight. She finished drinking and turned back. As she came to the edge of the clearing, the owl went over her again, and shortly afterwards there came the scream of a rabbit as the owl dropped on it.

The piercing cry, suddenly cutting across the silence of the evening, made her start. She stood looking toward it with her ears cocked for a moment and went on to circle downwind of the fawn to browse a little before she went to it. Fawns have no scent for a time, but soon a faint drift of fox came to her. It was the old dog fox which lived off the tract; he wandered widely now, for his mate had been shot by a farmer shortly before her pups were to be born. He was a danger to a very young fawn and, by the scent, was working his way into its vicinity. The doe snatched one mouthful of browse and moved quietly toward the fawn until she was close to but a little upwind of it, for the fox was coming upwind.

Not having the wind to favor him, he moved slowly, casting to one side of his line and then the other, often pausing to listen and look, ready to pounce on a young bird fallen from the nest, a beetle, or an easily confused young mouse. The fox would almost have to stumble over the fawn, for it kept very still.

He came nearer at a soft-footed pace that seemed leisurely but was not, for he was ready for a quick leap that would bring his forefeet or teeth down upon any hapless creature within reach. The doe, half concealed, was still; if the fox went by far enough away she wouldn't call attention to the fawn. Presently he appeared, on a course that would soon bring him upon the fawn, and the doe leaped from concealment to cut him up with her sharp forefeet.

The fox leaped sideways and fled and the doe pursued him, jumping rocks and fallen logs to get at him as he dodged about through the darkening woods, until finally he eluded her and galloped off. Satisfied that he had been driven away, she went back to the fawn.

First Pool was the longest of them all and even at low water in a dry summer was ten feet deep in the center. The stream slowed somewhat there and dropped some of the small amount of silt that it carried, and between this silt and the gravelly bottom it was a good place for many insects to deposit their eggs. The east bank was overhung with hemlocks and the west bank, five feet above the water, was a level little flood plain thick with brush; a good deal of the pool was in the sun several hours of the day, because there were few large trees on the west bank.

It was a very pretty pool, with Lower Falls at the head of it, and held some good trout, but there was a baseless feeling among the members that it was too close to the highway, too easily reached by the casual poacher, to hold much in the way of fish. Even Ohlmstead held this view and had never done much to prove it out, although he was always telling himself that he would the next time he went fishing. It was probably that he (and the other members as well) subconsciously wanted to avoid it because it was the closest pool to the road; they all wanted to get farther into the woods, away from anything that reminded them of civilization.

The afternoon was pleasant and cool, with a few high clouds and a light breeze from the west; whirligig beetles and water striders ran about on the water's surface in small backwaters near the shore. There were a few dragonflies which had escaped the spraying, gleaming like jewels, coursing above the stream or resting on their

hunting posts. They had emerged from the water a little earlier in the year, crawling up on the stem of a plant or a stick to split open their nymphal cases, dry their wings, and take to the air. For a time they had left the stream, coursing after their insect prey in the woods or the distant fields; they were beginning to return now to mate, and the males were picking out the territories they would defend against other males. They hadn't changed much in form in millions of years, for they were very efficient at their work, fast flyers which caught their prey in the basket of their legs. Their great compound eyes could detect motion at thirty feet or more. Their mating was peculiar. The male bent the tip of his abdomen forward and deposited his sperm in a copulatory organ there; he would find a female, catch her in his claspers, and as they flew about thus bound together she would bend her abdomen forward to reach the sperm. Their fertilized eggs would be deposited in the water; sometimes they would go beneath the surface together to do this.

On the bottom, among the stones, the nymphs of the yellow May fly, which had spent a year in their flattened, strange-looking nymphal form, were preparing to hatch. In their small bodies, seemingly so primitive and simple, they possessed an internal clock that told them it was time to leave the water; somehow they knew that the temperature and the humidity of the air were also right. After their long secretive life of burrowing in the silt and hiding beneath the stones, they must now expose themselves to all their enemies. There were thousands of them, for somehow, because of a fortunate eddy or current, they had escaped the effects of the spray in the water that had killed many other nymphs in the stream: suddenly they began, as though at a signal, to clamber from concealment and head for the surface.

As the current took them down, they swung a half circle upstream and rose; once upon the surface, they split their nymphal cases and rode upon them while their new wings dried and then flew up into the trees. A great many of them never got off the water, for as more and more of them appeared from the bottom, all the trout in the pool suddenly lost their usual caution and went mad to catch them, dashing about, breaking the surface, catching them on the rise or rising beneath them to suck them in, cramming their bellies with the great windfall of food. The water was torn and spray flew as the trout slashed at them; birds gathered as though by magic to gobble up those which had managed to get into the air. Thousands were eaten, but so many escaped that the air above the pool, as high as the treetops, was filled with their sulphur-yellow bodies and beating wings.

They got into the trees to conceal themselves and there would soon molt again and become more brilliant in color. In the evening they would fly again and mate and deposit their eggs on the water; then they would die. They wouldn't eat; they had no mouth parts to eat with; in a day or two they would be dead.

As suddenly as it had begun, the hatch was over. No more May flies came off the water, which flattened out and grew calm again as the gorged trout sank back to their usual stations. The air grew empty of May flies and the birds flew away. The frantic activity of a few minutes before had vanished as completely as though it had never been.

Farther up the stream, at the head of Eighth Pool, Ohlmstead was working the water with a spinner. He had fished his way up from the bridge and caught ten fish, putting back all but two. These two were natives, having hatched in the stream, and brilliantly colored; he never kept a stocked fish, and as he used a barb-less hook he could return them to the water unharmed. Had he known what had been going on at First Pool, he would have been considerably chagrined, not only because of the surprising number of trout there but also because he had always longed to be in on the excitement of such a bountiful hatch. Had he started in at First Pool, he would have been there at just the right time.

Unaware of what he had missed, he was enjoying himself. A kingfisher went noisily by as he cast into an eddy of foam near the dam, and he was at once fast to a sixteen-inch rainbow that was lying under it. Having been in the stream since the spring before, the fish started out strongly; it came out of the water and skittered across the surface on its tail, shaking its head wildly to dislodge the hook, and submerged again. Ohlmstead thought that he was going to have his hands full for a time, but then the fish turned loggy. He netted it and, not liking rainbows to eat, released it; it had been a disappointing fish and he wondered why.

He climbed out of the pool and as he was cutting across through the woods to S Pool walked into a brood of young grouse. It seemed to be a very small brood, from what he could see of it; usually there were many more at this time. The old bird went up with a roar, and the young scattered in all directions. They weren't old enough to fly very far and all but one came down within a few feet to hide in the brush; one of them managed to reach the stream and fall into it. Ohlmstead saw it and went after it, but by the time he had got it out of the water it had drowned. He held it in his hand re-gretfully, for he hated to see one of such a small brood dead, and as he was looking at the wet little body he suddenly realized that he was going to use it to try to catch the old trout in Upper Falls Pool.

He hadn't planned to fish for it today; rather, he had planned not to. He had been thinking of it a good deal, usually after he got into bed at night, and had enjoyed these meditations and the mental pictures they brought him, his feelings of excitement and anticipation, so much that he had put off going after the fish. Also, because of the almost insurmountable difficulty of using a fly or a spinner in the pool, he would have to use bait, and he didn't like bait-fishing; brought to it, he hadn't been able to think of a bait he wanted to use. As he went down the list of frogs, worms, mice, salmon eggs, and whatnot, he had decided against them all. He had been pretty whimsical about the trout, and he grew more whimsical still; he decided that such a fish, if it was going to be caught on bait, would have to be caught on bait that no one he'd ever heard about had ever used.

Now that he had it and the encounter couldn't be put off any longer, he walked back to his car, which was parked near the bridge, and drove up to the end of the road. He took off his waders, for they would only be a hazard in the procedure he had in mind, put on his sneakers, tied a hook instead of a spinner to the end of his line, and walked through the woods to the top of the ledge above Upper Falls Pool. It was still early; the falls and the pool were still in shadow, and as he looked down on the dark water and the secrets it held, the excitement he had managed to control built up in him. With fingers that shook a little, he carefully put the baby grouse on the hook.

His plan was to crawl partway down the ledge, where he would still be concealed, cast the grouse into the falls, and let it wash down into the pool on a rather loose line. If the trout took it and was hooked, he might be able to hang on to it until he could work himself low enough on the ledge to play and net it. It was, as he had admitted to himself when he first thought of it, a fool plan, as crazy as something a kid would cook up, and about as likely to succeed; it was so crazy that it fascinated him.

With his back to the rock and his free hand overhead grasping projections of the ledge, he slid down to a precarious foothold and steadied himself. The ledge below looked pretty precipitous, but he was sure he could manage it; he wasn't going to back out now. "Well," he said to himself, "here goes." He made the cast.

The baby grouse landed nicely on top of the waterfall, washed over, and vanished into the white water below; Ohlmstead took in a little line, and almost immediately there was a tremendous strike. The rod bent almost double; the trout felt the hook and made for his retreat beneath the ledge across the stream with such sudden and unexpected power that Ohlmstead was overbalanced. He clawed wildly about, lost his footing, and fell into the pool with a great splash.

The cold water took his breath, and after thrashing about he got straightened away and swam to the end of the pool and scrambled out, soaked and shivering, still holding his rod. The line was limp; it had broken on the sharp corner of the rock when the trout ran into one of the fissures under the ledge.

Ohlmstead raised his left hand in salute toward the head of the pool and grinned a lopsided grin. "Hail and maybe farewell!" he said, between chattering teeth, and turned for his car.

The red-spotted newt (called a red eft during her life on land), a reddish-brown little amphibian with bright red spots and golden eyes, was returning to the stream again to resume her life in the water, mate, and lay her eggs. She had been hatched in the stream three years before from an egg deposited on the stem of an underwater plant, and for a time had lived as a larva with gills; after she had developed lungs she had climbed out of the water and begun to wander about catching small insects and eventually reached the bog where the doe went to drink while her fawn was very small.

The eft was only about three inches long and her legs were fragile and weak; she was a delicate and dainty creature, small and slow-moving, and the bog was over a mile from the stream. It had been an immense journey for her and full of peril, for she had many enemies and couldn't escape them by flight. She had to make her way among the fallen leaves and cracks between the rocks, a slow and tortuous process, and avoid the heat of the day in cool, damp spots beneath stones or in the humus beneath the ground's surface layer, for she dried out quickly and drying out would kill her.

She had left the vicinity of the bog in late summer the year before, starting her long journey back toward the stream and the spring run where she had hatched. She moved with an extraordinary sureness of direction; she hadn't been near the stream for over two years and during that time had felt no inclination for it, but now, even if she had been blinded, she would have found her way. Winter's snow had stopped her and she had gone underground, pushing her way down to join the myriads of mites, insect larvae, worms, spiders, ants, centipedes, and other creatures that slept the cold time away, but as soon as the path was open again she had worked her way to the surface and started off.

The long winter had delayed her, but finally, while the last of the wild azalea was blossoming in the woods, she reached the pool in the spring run where she had first seen the light of day. It was a pretty little pool, ten feet across, bounded by rocks and moss and shadowed by hemlocks, with a tiny waterfall at each end, and she dropped into it just before a garter snake, hunting along the bank, could strike at her, and left forever the land upon which she had wandered for so long.

There were rocks and drifts of old leaves scattered about on the sandy bottom and she moved about among them; the second day she was there a male salamander crawled around the edge of one of the rocks and they saw each other at the same time. He became agitated and then began a stealthy approach to her, but she darted away. He pursued her a short distance and then began another stealthy approach, perfectly obvious in the clear water. Again she darted away, and for a time their game went on until she relented and allowed him to come nearer. At this sign of acquiescence he thrashed about and vaulted upon her and, clasping her around the body with his hind legs, moved up until he had her around the throat in so tight a grip that she was immobilized and helpless. They were quiet for a time, then the male began to swing his tail rhythmically from side to side and the female slowly raised hers. This excited him so much that he became quite violent and for ten minutes pulled and jerked her wildly about, then left her and went through a series of strenuous undulations; the female followed him and pressed her head against his tail and he deposited a spermatophore. This was a flat disc from which arose a spinelike structure holding a spherical mass of spermatozoa at its tip, and the female moved over it and pressed her cloaca against it and was fertilized.

From this strange mating she would presently begin to lay a series of single eggs, a few a day, attaching them to submerged plant stems or rocks; the egg-laying would be a long-drawn-out affair until possibly several hundred eggs were laid. When the larvae hatched they would be a little over half an inch long, light yellow-green, with gills and front leg buds that would rapidly elongate; in about eighty-four days they would be full grown, looking like little tadpoles. The wide fins on their tails would disappear; they would lose their gills and finally climb out on shore to change color and wander about until they were mature, just as she had done, and then return to the water again. They would be active most of the year, crawling slowly about on the bottom, eating small worms and other amphibians and their eggs, and insects, burying themselves in the bottom mud when the water was at its coldest. In their permanent water life they would keep their red spots, but their reddish-brown color would turn to green.

Late in the afternoon an overcast moved across the sky, darkening the golden patches of sunlight in the shadowy woods; distant thunder grumbled, and presently it began to rain. At first the rain was light, pattering softly on the leaves, but all sentient life seemed to know that it would grow heavier and took cover. The storm moved closer. Lightning ripped across the sky, thunder shook the earth, and a roaring curtain of big raindrops brought visibility down to a few yards. The storm wind, violent and cold, whipped the trees and brought many branches down and many nests and young birds with them. They were battered to death or killed in falling, or drowned in the rain pools or little rills rushing down from higher ground. Porous as the forest floor was, it couldn't soak up all of such a rain as fast as it fell. The stream's song changed and deepened as it rose higher and more of the spray remaining on the ground washed into it.

The storm ended near sundown, and a chilly mist arose and swirled languidly through the soaked and darkening woods; later the moon shone eerily upon it. The aisles between the trees, and brush, drew in to secret, misty labyrinths. An old male skunk from higher up the ridge, whose mate had six new young and had cast him out, had wandered out of his own rather small territory and was at loose ends until at some time in the future he might be allowed to join the family again. He now started down toward the stream. He had not been long on the way when he stumbled upon a dead young wood thrush, which was pleasant; his diet, largely of insects, had been reduced since the spraying. A bit later he found a young yellow-breasted chat. These two little victims of the storm pretty well filled his belly. Ordinarily he would have turned back up the ridge, but the spirit of exploration came upon him and he continued down the stream. He reached it at Sixth Pool; he had never seen the stream before and for a time stared at the brawling water. He wanted to get closer to it, but its roaring force made him pause. He finally decided not to get closer to it and started down-stream on the path the fishermen used. He crossed the spring run between Fifth and Sixth Pools, and the scent of yellow jackets came to him and he moved a few feet off the path and found their hole in the ground. He was very fond of yellow jackets and their larvae, and began to dig for them. In the daytime they would have swarmed all over him, but the darkness and the chill immobilized them and he cleaned out the colony, thus saving from pain and sorrow some fisherman who would have stepped a little way off the path.

Comfortably full now, he went on and between Fourth and Fifth Pools began to hear fragmentary sounds of altercation above the noise of the stream. The mist cut off his view beyond a few yards, but that didn't concern him; there were very few creatures for which he would step aside, and he marched on. The snarling and growling before him grew louder, and in several more yards he came upon two pairs of raccoon—one from the old beech in Bear Swamp and another from farther down the stream—which had encountered one another and had been quarreling for nearly an hour. They both wanted to hunt that part of the stream, for the bank was low and the water was shallow and easily worked, and the Bear Swamp raccoons considered it their territory. The females were threatening each other with short rushes and the males were recovering their breath from a recent battle and preparing for another one. Their young were still a little too small to be out, and were at home in the dens. The uproar was considerable and the skunk, seeing so many of them in his way, paused for a moment. They all saw him at about the same time. Their snarling stopped and they all faced him, their fur standing up with rage, their eyes glowing; and their systems, full of adrenaline, were further angered by an interloper who seemed to want to interfere with their private affair; they weren't in a mood for discretion. They showed him their teeth and then looked at one another. A common cause was born in the look. They began to growl again and swung sideways to move up on him.

Two of them meant no more than one to the skunk, and retreat never entered his mind; he turned quickly about and raised his tail in warning. The Bear Swamp raccoon in his youth had had experience with this banner of impending disaster and was immediately recalled to it; he turned tail and left the field, driving his mate before him. They were just out of range when the other raccoon, too wrathful to be prudent, kept on and suffered the consequences. The skunk's spray, mephitic and faintly luminous in the moonlight mist, caught him full in the face; he was blinded and half asphyxiated, and rolled about on the ground in agony. His mate was farther away and suffered less, but she turned and fled down the path.

Left in command of the reeking battlefield, the skunk made a half circle around the thrashing raccoon and continued on his way, picking up his pace until he got to cleaner air. Then he slowed again, but continued on the path until he passed Third Pool and came to the bridge. It was a new thing to him and he looked it over carefully before he crossed it, pausing in the middle to survey the stream below. On the other side he followed the road for a few feet and then turned off to the northeast toward Bear Swamp and presently came to the spring run.

The run wound about and the banks, continually watered and receiving a fair amount of sun, were grassy and well grown with wild iris and other plants; the female porcupine which lived in a shallow cave near the edge of the swamp fed there during the late spring and summer. With her she had the young one that had been born in May. It had been born with its eyes open, its incisor teeth rather well developed, and had been able to walk within an hour; as soon as it had dried, its little quills were hard and sharp.

Soon it was going abroad with its mother, and while it was still nursing, it was already sampling almost every plant that grew, and learning to climb. As they moved about, they were seldom close together. The baby sometimes went out independently, but when they were out together their courses were roughly parallel, for they had some mysterious method of communication with each other.

When he was halfway to the spring where the run began, the skunk came upon the old porcupine moving in his direction. She was going slowly, nibbling at plants and young shrubs along the faint path that she had made; the skunk was also in the path, and she stopped feeding when she saw him. The skunk stopped too, for although he wasn't inclined to move aside he had before him an opponent that he didn't know. He had never seen a porcupine in his home territory and was a little wary of this one.

For a short time the two of them, each armored with a different but fearsome weapon, eyed each other. Neither of them was particularly intelligent, for there were few occasions in their lives or the lives of their ancestors which called for intelligence, and their weapons were defensive; if one of them got out of character and attacked, he would get the worst of it. As it turned out, the deadlock was broken by the young porcupine a few yards away off the path; it fell into a shallow hole between two rocks and raised its squeaky voice in lamentation. The old one moved off toward it, and the skunk took up his way along the path.

The land rose gently as he followed the winding spring run, catching a red eft on the path a few inches from the water that was its destination; a little farther on, he passed within a few yards of a grouse brooding her four small young, without knowing she was there. As the rising ground took him higher above the run the mist

thinned out and the moonlight slanting through an opening gleamed on the broad white stripes along his sides and on his tail, which was almost pure white.

The female horned owl from the nest near Upper Falls was sitting high in a dead chestnut farther up the hill; she had missed a flying squirrel not long before and had taken perch in the chestnut facing away from the skunk, but as her head swiveled about to scan the ground below (for her eyes were fixed in their sockets), she saw the moving gleam of white and turned on the limb to face it. She had caught nothing, for the mist had blanked off the ground and the soaked forest floor had deadened the sounds of the creatures which stirred about on it, and she was hungry.

The skunk's course was bringing him in her direction, and she watched until he came close enough to be clearly seen; then, silent as a ghost, she swooped down on him, took him in the head and loin, and ended his adventure.

His home territory would be the poorer without him, for although he had taken his toll of the eggs of ground-nesting birds, he had been less dangerous to them than a raccoon; his diet had been mostly insects and he had been valuable in keeping them in check. He had been in the main an inoffensive creature except when threatened or met on the trail, which he thought belonged to him, and this small arrogance was not without its dangers; it wasn't good to be heedless or overconfident in his world.

T W O

In ADDITION TO writing to Goodenow, Ohlmstead had talked about the survey crew to several of the other members he met on the stream, and the upshot of all this was some quiet investigation in the state capital, where two of the members had business connections. One of these men, whose name was MacDonald, stopped at Ohlmstead's house the next time he came fishing.

"Morning, Jerry," he said, when Ohlmstead came to the door. "I thought I'd stop in and give you a rundown on what we found out about the survey."

"Hi, Mac," Ohlmstead said. "Come in and have some coffee. I'm just on my second cup. You must have got up early this morning."

"Well, I woke up about four and it looked like such a nice day I decided to sneak off," MacDonald said, and followed Ohlmstead into the breakfast room. He sat down while Ohlmstead went for another cup and saucer, and lit a cigarette while Ohlmstead poured the coffee for him. "Good coffee," he said, drinking some. "Our water's so full of chlorine at home it's not fit to drink."

"My housekeeper fixes it before she leaves at night. All I have to do is plug it in. Would you like a couple of eggs?"

"No, thanks, I've had breakfast. How's the fishing been?"

"Oh, you'll catch some fish. There aren't as many bugs since the spraying, and they're hungry. I've been doing well with a Mickey Finn, but a lot of the fish seem to give up without much of a scuffle. Maybe that's the spraying too, but we can't fix that now; we can only hope the results are temporary. I wrote to Alec and suggested he tell the state to keep the spray where it belongs, and I hope he's done it. What did you find out about the survey?"

"Well," MacDonald said, "from what we can find out, it looks like they're thinking of putting a lake in on that little state park a couple of miles above our line, and a new road to it."

"There's a road to it already," Ohlmstead said.

"I know, the one up the river. But they think they'll get more people to go there if there's a lake to fish in, and that it would be easier to get to it from here if there was another road."

"Road builders," Ohlmstead said, "have to keep on building roads, damn it. They set up an organization and then expand it and have to keep on finding things for it to do. The whole country's turning into a slab of concrete. I don't much like the idea of a lake up there either; it might warm up the stream or change the water table or whatever, but I guess if they've decided on a lake we'll get a lake. Anyhow, if anybody wanted to fish in this lake, and was willing to go to a little trouble to do it, they wouldn't mind driving the extra five or six miles to get to it on the old road. Why the devil do things have to be made easier for people who get lazier all the time, without any consideration of what the effects may be? If they put a new road where those guys were going to survey, it'll be right on the ridge line, and we'll get the erosion from it; so will the stream below us, and the river. Besides that, if there's a new road somebody will start a development up there and we'll get the sewage from that."

"I know it. I don't think the new road's necessary or even indicated for a long time to come. The way things are going, there will be a development, and some of it will be on the strip we own on our side of the road, for the best view's from there. They'll have to treat the sewage, but there'll be a lot of nitrogen and phosphorus and things like that coming down into the stream that will change the water and probably give us more algae."

They were both silent for a long moment, and then Ohlmstead went on: "You said, the way things are going, there'll be a development. What makes you think that?"

"Well, after we found out about the lake, four or five of us got to talking. We wondered if we could buy the strip on our side of the road, to keep the development on the other side so the sewage would drain that way. Buy it before the word got out, that is, and the price went out of sight."

"And?" Ohlmstead asked.

MacDonald shook his head. "The word's already got out. Either that, or there's been a deal somewhere. It's not for sale, unless we all turn into millionaires. A couple of years ago it could have been picked up for fifty an acre. Now a thousand wouldn't touch it."

"We should have had a crystal ball," Ohlmstead said.

"It's been going on ever since early in the century," MacDonald said. "The country's best nesting grounds for ducks on the prairies —which were swamps never meant for farming—were drained and the land sold to the innocent, who found they couldn't farm it, so it was ruined because some developer got together with some politico for a fast buck. I had an uncle who was caught in one of those deals. In our case, we're just caught with an unnecessary road. As usual, it was done very quietly."

"So it seems," Ohlmstead said. "Hell. Another cup of coffee?"

"No, thanks, Jerry. I'd better mosey along if I want to get some fishing in."

"Come to dinner," Ohlmstead said.

"Well, thanks, but I'd better get home when I'm through fishing."

"Why? You can't fish all day on a couple of sandwiches your wife packed for you and then drive home. You'd have to stop somewhere to eat. I'd like it if you came."

MacDonald smiled. "All right. I'd like to."

"See you at seven, then. Have a good day."

MacDonald sketched a salute and went out. Ohlmstead watched him get into his car and drive off, and went back to the breakfast room. He sat down and poured another cup of coffee but didn't drink it right away. MacDonald's news had upset him, and he sat staring out the window as he thought of it. His notion that this might be the year when things began to close in on them, which he had dismissed as crepe-hanging at the time, came back to him. Misfortunes seldom came singly, and there could be more; basically they would be related. What else was going to happen?

It was inevitable, as time and the population explosion went on and more people sought places to escape their own self-imposed clutter and uproar, that the stream and the land around it would be increasingly hedged in and disturbed; it wasn't within their power to prevent it.

They had been fortunate so far, but their good fortune wouldn't last forever, and the pace of change was accelerating. Dams changed the drainage patterns and water tables of the areas around them, and who knew what the effects of the new lake above them would be? Would it warm the water enough to change the stream's ecology, and in dry summers would it hold back too much water from the stream? And the new road: if it was properly graded and built and the banks properly planted, the erosion might be temporary, but there would be other and equally unnecessary roads; every acre they covered up with concrete kept water from seeping down into the underground water table and added to the rapid run-off that caused floods—which meant more dams.

Sooner or later they would be surrounded, and there would be more roads, more erosion, more sewage. It would be treated—in a measure, as MacDonald had said—but things wouldn't be the same. Ohlmstead's heart sank as he thought of the present clear, clean water, for he had followed the history of too many rivers and streams which had been befouled beyond all bearing to increase somebody's profit, when for a little less profit the befoulment could be controlled.

Ohlmstead wasn't a selfish man, nor foolish enough to want to turn the clock back; neither did he wish to exclude people from the natural world. It was part of their heritage, they needed it more than ever before and deserved it as much as he did; the heedless and destructive way in which they used it was what caused his apprehension and distress. Naturally, he didn't want careless people running about on or changing for the worse what he fancifully called "our little Eden," for on top of their larger transgressions against nature they always seemed to demolish the flora and leave their litter where they were finished with it. The tract, aside from his love for it, was a symbol, a microcosm—quiet, carefully managed to avoid unnecessary disturbance, beautiful, and in balance—of what the world beyond it should be. He was always ready to point this out to anyone who called him a nature crank for his views; he didn't care if it made him unpopular with some people, so long as it induced them to think. "Nature nourishes you," he would say. "Who will do it when you have finally managed to demolish her?"

The wild grapes had finished their fragrant blooming, with the fox grapes the most fragrant of all, and the blossoms of the May apples had long fallen; the leaves of the oaks were fully out, bringing more shade to the forest floor. The laurel opened its flowers; the tips of the stamens were held under tension, so that the slightest jar when an insect landed on them released them, and like miniature catapults they sprang up and scattered their pollen. They were more numerous near the quaking bog on the ridge, where they made a big, almost impenetrable thicket twelve feet high liked by the grouse. Rhododendrons blossomed and brought their color to the stream, flowering along its banks in their greatest number near S Pool among the gray rock ledges and dark hemlocks. Worker bumblebees, butterflies, and other nectar-sipping insects were busy among them all, and many kinds of pollen floated invisibly on the air.

As the days grew warmer the voices of the tract's surviving insects increased in volume; many that cried out were unheard by other creatures because their love songs were of too high a pitch. Crickets chirped and cicadas sang their long, grating songs. They had emerged at the end of May; now they were winged and adult and presently would mate and lay their eggs. Sometimes their song would be ended in a discordant screech as a female king hornet, the cicada killer, located them by their singing and fell upon them. Struggling together, they would drop to the ground and the hornet would locate a vital spot and paralyze her victim with a sting, then take it off to a hole she had dug and lay an egg on it beneath the middle leg. The egg would hatch, the larva would eat the living but paralyzed cicada, spin a cocoon, and wait until the following spring to develop into an adult.

The coolness of the nights would silence the cicadas that escaped the hornets, but the crickets would continue their songs and so would the katydids. The males of these long-horned grasshoppers did their singing by rubbing the ridges on one wing cover back and forth across the rasps on the other; the females heard them with the ears on their front legs. They would mate at the end of summer; sometimes the male would have his head bitten off as they mated. The young would emerge the following spring and voraciously attack plant lice and other pests; by late summer they would be fully grown and have wings.

Besides these noisy insects there were millions that were silent or made ultrasonic sounds audible only to their own species, or released far-carrying scents by which their mates found them, or glowed in the dark; the pollenizers, the destroyers, and those that fed upon them both, aided by a great segment of the vertebrate world, were a vastly complicated and interdependent network of life. Some were catholic in their requirements but others were so specialized, pursuing a single prey species, that control measures which were careless or used without sufficient knowledge, allowing that prey a disastrous irruption, could take away the livelihood of others and bring them down. Both of these things had happened on the tract, and only time would show the results of it.

As the cubs increased in size and strength, the old bear had gradually increased her range. Although there were people in the woods along the stream and the roads, she found extremely few of them in other places and stayed mostly in these places; inevitably she encountered scents from the village dump and several outlying farmhouses, and as these scents were very enticing she presently began to investigate them. She did this very carefully, taking a good deal of time to circle them from a distance and assay their possible danger with her nose and ears, which were as keen as any animal's in the forest. One by one the farmhouses were discovered to have dogs, as they had had in the past, and one by one she turned away from them; but there were no dogs at the dump and she finally led the cubs to it.

She had a little trouble keeping them from running heedlessly to it from a long way off, for the new and wonderful scents excited them, but with a forepaw heavier than usual she finally curbed them into following her in single file in a vigilant and circuitous approach. Once they were there, three darker shadows in the starry darkness of the night, the cubs found a turkey carcass and fell to scuffling fiercely over it. The rats of the dump, which had withdrawn to their observation posts when the bears came in, withdrew farther, and the old bear, nervous on her first visit, smacked the cubs apart, picked up the carcass in her mouth, and made off with it. The cubs each grabbed something and followed her. One of them had a greasy piece of metal foil and the other a bone from a leg of lamb; when they were far enough in the woods to suit the old bear they all went to work on their prizes.

Because their first foray had been successful, they made a habit of returning at intervals, and as nothing disturbed them they spent more time and were more selective, but the old bear never brought them twice from the same direction and always made them carry their loot away and eat it in the woods. They sometimes encountered foraging skunks or raccoons, snakes or a weasel or a fox hunting rats or an occasional owl there for the same purpose; once there was a barn owl, which lived in a dank tree hollow that never dried out near the village and which was faintly luminous from the fungus that grew in its abode. The bird was sitting on top of a pile of trash with its back to the bears one night when they came silently in, and the cubs had a moment to be startled by its dim eerie glow before it flapped off. They retreated a little way; they had often watched fireflies, the males flashing their lights in the air to be answered by the waiting females in the grass, but this creature was large and different. In its shape it reminded them of the horned owls that had attacked them near Upper Falls, and for that night they wouldn't follow the old bear into the dump but moved whining around the perimeter of it.

For a time after this encounter they looked for the owl when they approached the dump, but they didn't see it again. They gradually grew less apprehensive, and nothing else disturbed them until late one Sunday afternoon so cloudy and dark that they went to the dump several hours before their usual time. Two of the village boys were there with their .22 caliber rifles to shoot rats; they were downwind and sitting quietly under a hemlock and had not been discovered because the old bear had grown a little careless and for once neglected her usual exploratory approach. The bears appeared so silently and unexpectedly before the boys that they were startled and jumped up, revealing themselves only a few yards away.

The old bear was as startled as the boys, and confused. Their proximity and sudden, jerky movements came very close to looking like an attack and she couldn't turn her back on it; she rose on her hind legs, growling, and the cubs ran behind her. She looked very big and threatening, and the boys were badly frightened. They drew together and stared at her, half raised their rifles, and for a dangerous moment were almost panicked into shooting. If the bear had moved a step or two toward them they probably would have done it, but she made no attempt to move on them and they had time to realize how inadequate their rifles were. "Let's get out of here," one of them said, and they turned and fled. Seeing this, the bear dropped to all fours, whirled about, and driving the cubs before her vanished in the opposite direction.

The old bear pushed the cubs along until they were in the swamp which drained into Hemlock Pool, and even there, in the dense, quiet shade of the hemlocks, she wasn't at ease; when one of the cubs fell to playing with a cardinal flower, brilliant red on its tall spike, she cuffed them both and decided to put more distance between them all and the dump. She grunted to the cubs and started on a course that would parallel the stream until they were near the tract's northern boundary, where they could cross by jumping from rock to rock.

Once across the stream, the old bear felt a little safer, as though she had put a barrier between herself and the boys, and she slowed her pace and set a course across the rising ground toward the quaking bog on the ridge. The warm summer night held the stridulations of katydids and the monotonous chorale of tree crickets, which synchronized with one another; an occasional beetle blundered by, and one of the cubs found a Luna moth clinging to a tree, its body swollen with eggs and its lovely wings battered after its mating flight. His paw flattened bedraggled beauty against the bark; in the morning the ants and carrion flies would find it.

He caught up with the others as they moved slowly along, digging roots and eating plants that seemed good to them, tearing stumps and rotting logs apart for grubs, finding a yellow-jacket nest or two to dig into. A doe with two fawns snorted at them and moved off; the deer scent was only one thread of a skein of scents, entwined, greatly varied, fading or growing stronger as they moved —a better and more revealing guide than sight to what was in the segment of the world upwind of them. Here a shrew had gone by, a tiny, ill-smelling embodiment of hunger-driven fury ready to attack mouse, insect, or anything else it could master; here a rabbit had crouched in its forme through the day and was now gone foraging; here a chipmunk burrow gave off the scent of the sleeper far down in its labyrinth among the roots and rocks. The low-bush blueberries scattered through the woods were ripening their fruit and the bears gleaned what the birds, chipmunks, mice, and squirrels had left, but the old bear knew from the past that the high-bush blue-berries around the bog were better and larger and continued on in that direction. She would have gone there before if she hadn't been seduced by the dump and stayed in that vicinity for a time; she wouldn't go back again.

When they got near the bog the old bear, not to be caught by carelessness again, circled it before moving into the dry area around the bog's edge where the blueberries grew. Halfway around she heard a rabbit scream; coming back almost to her starting point, she caught the scent of blood, rabbit, and weasel, and following them came to the weasel crouched over the rabbit he had killed. The cubs had been behind her but had caught the scent too and began to move past her. She ordered them back; they knew nothing of weasels and their capabilities. They sat down and watched her, cocking their heads.

The old bear moved closer, taking her time and almost seeming to make a game of it, and the weasel, which had been crouched watchfully behind the rabbit's body, put his forefeet on it and snarled at her. He was undecided for the moment whether to stand or retreat, and then took hold of the rabbit and began to drag it off. The bear moved again, cutting down the distance between them, pushing him into a decision; she knew she probably couldn't catch him, for he could dodge about with remarkable quickness, and she wanted him to attack. He dropped the rabbit and faced her again despite the vast difference in their sizes, screeching with rage, his eyes glowing green, and when she moved as though to pounce at him he leaped for her throat. He was as quick as a striking snake, but the bear was quick too; her rising paw deflected him upward, and his teeth caught her lower lip instead of her throat. She flipped him up, her jaws closed on him, and his screeching stopped; she had brought him to disaster by using his own mad courage against him.

She pulled him off her lip, discarded him because of his skunk-like scent gland that is common to all weasels, and shared the rabbit with the cubs before they headed for the blueberries.

The surviving young horned owl, after a period of growing that stretched over many weeks, had got on the wing; after flying short distances from branch to branch for a time, overshooting or under-shooting his mark and clumsily flapping and teetering back and forth, he had acquired enough confidence and skill to follow his parents about. They had taken good care of him, fed him, showed him how they hunted, but not all the young of predatory birds begin to hunt at the same time; some are later than others, and he was one of them. Although most horned owls are patient and at-tend their young for a long time, the old pair were getting weary of him; they relaxed their watchfulness and as often as they could get out of his sight avoided him. This wasn't easy, for he preferred to be fed rather than shift for himself, and clung closely to one or the other of them, making loud, harsh, blood-curdling screams charac-teristic of young horned owls.

Presently, however, he did begin to grapple with prey that the old owls caught while there was still a little life in it, and the predator's fierce joy in the kill entered into him; thereafter, although he still screamed to be fed, he began to hunt for himself. When he caught his first young rabbit, dropping on it in an opening where he was hunting with his mother at dusk, he dug in his talons, propped

himself with his wings, and, wild-eyed and with snapping beak, puffed up in self-congratulation. He had learned the essential lesson, and the old birds didn't fail to observe it.

The next time he caught a young rabbit he was hunting with his mother again, near the quaking bog on the ridge, and while he was concentrating on it the old owl slipped away. Not long before, she had heard her mate hoot near the stream, and went looking for him. She did not find him quickly so she hooted and was answered from upstream; she flew that way, hooting again, and found him on a high dead branch of a tall oak and landed next to him. They bowed and looked at one another; the female gave a soft "Ank? Ank? Ank?" and flew off toward the east, returning again when the male didn't follow her. She landed once more, gave a soft, high-pitched call again, and again left the branch. This time the male followed her, and they flew together over the ridge toward the river.

After the rabbit had ceased twitching, the young owl flew with it to the top of a lichened rock nearby, plucked most of the fur from it and ate it, scraped his beak clean on the rock, shook his feathers into place, and sat looking around for a time. He didn't know where his mother was and listened for her voice, but his crop was full of meat and he wasn't much concerned for the moment. He sat on, occasionally stretching and twisting his neck to move more meat from his crop to his stomach, listening to the sounds of the night. His hearing, like that of all owls, was very keen and his ears were asymmetrical; they gave two slightly different responses to sounds that enabled him to pinpoint them with extraordinary accuracy, and he could catch things that he couldn't see, if they made the faintest stirring.

Several hours went by, while mice scuttled through their runways and beetles lumbered past; he heard a rabbit thump and a deer feeding across the bog, but he didn't hear his parents. Later in the night he began to feel lonely, for he had never been alone for very long, and presently gave several screams. They weren't answered, and he shuffled about on top of the rock in indecision. A screech owl came by and seeing him swung swiftly away, put on speed, and vanished; he took off from the rock and flew to the vicinity of the old nest, perched near it, and screamed again. There still was no answer and he flew up and down the stream for a time, perching occasionally to scream with increasing vigor and uneasiness. Dawn found him still searching, and an early-stirring crow that spotted him and gave tongue to call its friends together for a mobbing sent him into a dense stand of hemlocks to hide for the rest of the day. For a time, while the crows wheeled about screaming and searching for him, he stood with his body elongated and his eyes closed on a branch, pressed against the tree's trunk; finally the crows lost interest in their enterprise and drifted off one by one, leaving him to the lonely day.

He had a voracious appetite and was accustomed to being well fed by his parents; he was hungry before evening, and although he could have hunted by daylight he stayed in hiding to avoid the crows, for he couldn't face them with the equanimity of the old owls. Early dusk found him moving again after a restless and lonely day during which he napped uneasily between periods of listening and peering about. He visited the places where the old owls had spent their resting time and the trees to which they had often carried their prey to eat, screaming for them, but hunger finally drove him to give up his fruitless search and hunt.

Wheeling his way through the darkening woods, he missed a cock grouse belatedly going to roost, and finally came to the edge of the bog and perched on top of a stone. The stars were beginning to appear and a bank of clouds to the west held the last fading and diffused color of the sunken sun; he heard a stirring in the dry leaves below the concealing cover of the low brush and dropped on it although the sound pattern was unfamiliar. It was a big black snake following a mouse trail, and his talons went around instead of through it; he had been careless in his hungry haste and ignorance and caught it too far forward. In a flash the snake had a coil around him and as swiftly began to tighten it and attempt to throw a second coil. Although the owl's legs were pinioned his wings were not, and he flopped wildly about, trying to get his talons free, rolling over and over and rising in short erratic flights and falling again. His grip around the snake's neck was choking it but not quickly enough and the coil was crushing him. Horned owls kill with their feet, but in his extremity he began to bite at it desperately, and more by luck than by design, bit its head off. The coils relaxed and he got out of them to stagger off a little way and sit panting and exhausted for a long time before he came back to the snake and ate it. He had been bruised and lost some feathers, besides being badly frightened; he was fortunate that he hadn't been killed.

He had been so badly battered about and alarmed by the encounter that after he finished the snake he flew up to the rock from which he had dropped on it and sat for several hours before moving again. It was full dark now, and the owl finally left the rock and flew through the woods to the nest, threading his way through the trees as easily as though it was full daylight. He saw several does and their fawns and chased a flying squirrel that eluded him by spiraling swiftly around the trunk of a beech and popping into a hole. The old owls were nowhere about, but this time he didn't scream for them; he was beginning to adjust to their absence, to realize somehow that he wouldn't find them again. If they had stayed with him longer they would eventually have driven him off anyhow, for the territory they had held (and would possibly return to in time) couldn't continue to support the three of them. In fact, it would hardly support him now; it needed a rest if the game was to bring up its numbers again, for it had been overhunted, and this was probably one of the reasons the old owls had abandoned it.

Within the next few nights the young owl, who had been fortunate at first in making several kills for himself, found this out. Only the wariest creatures, the most difficult to catch, were left, and he couldn't catch any more of them. He was forced to go farther and farther afield, and although he wanted to stay in the vicinity of the nest he finally found it too far to return and gave it up. He wandered about for a time and presently settled on an area about ten miles west of the stream on a plateau where there were hemlock, second-growth oaks, and big laurel thickets interspersed with three or four farms.

The hunting was good; there were many rabbits and a few grouse around the edges of the fields, but one of the farmers raised chickens, which he sold in the village, and as he let the chickens range, the owl found them easy to catch and caught too many of them. The farmer thought at first that a fox was robbing him, but late one afternoon he saw the owl take a chicken near the edge of the woods, and he set up a pole with a steel trap on top of it. The

next evening the owl landed on the pole and was caught by one leg.

The clang of the trap and its sudden iron grip were terrifying; the owl leaped away but was pulled up short by the trap chain to hang head down beside the pole, flapping desperately with all his strength to try to get away and fight the thing that held him. After his first blind panic he sank the talons of his free foot into the pole and pulled against the chain with the trapped leg and was strong enough to pull out the staple that held the trap chain and fly off with the trap.

Once in the woods, he came to the ground and rolled about fighting the trap, repeatedly striking at it and hissing and growling with rage, but the steel was impervious to his talons; finally he was reduced to exhaustion and had to accept the thing that held him, stumping about and dragging the chain. After he recovered from his first struggles he had fits of fighting with the trap but finally gave them up, though flying and landing in trees with the heavy, clogging trap and the dangling chain that whipped around branches and caught on things gave him a great deal of trouble and pain.

Besides the trouble the trap and the chain gave him in getting about, they interfered with his hunting, and despite his inclination to avoid the vicinity where he had been caught he was driven back to the chickens again, for they were easy to catch or snatch out of the trees in which they roosted. He took several and the farmer put another trap on the pole, but he avoided it; the farmer then shut his chickens up, with the exception of two, which he tethered out in the evenings near a clump of hemlocks in which he could hide with a shotgun. After many hours of patient waiting the man finally got a shot, but it was nearly dark and the swooping owl made a difficult target. Several pellets shaved his skin and took out some feathers, leaving him unharmed, but the fiery, roaring blast of the gun and the shock of the pellets that could have killed him frightened him so much that he fled the place and flew for several miles before perching in a tree beside the highway.

Two cars went by beneath him, great noisy things behind swiftly moving cones of light; the third one stopped a short distance beyond him for a moment and then went on. The people in it had dropped out a half-grown cat to shift for itself, having grown tired of it, and the owl saw it standing uncertainly at the edge of the road and swooped down upon it. With only one usable foot, which had caught the cat across the shoulders, he had a hard time managing it as it fought desperately for its life. They were struggling in the middle of the road when another car came swiftly along in a flare of blinding light and killed them both.

The poacher, Slattery, had been out of sorts all day; he didn't get out of his dirty blankets until lunchtime, and then a pain in his chest began that lasted most of the afternoon and had finally extended into his left arm before it went away, leaving him feeling dizzy and short of breath. He hadn't eaten any breakfast or lunch, but two hours before sundown he began to feel hungry and found that there was nothing in the shack to eat, so he pulled on a pair of Levi's and a shirt and walked to the village to buy a can or two of beans. He didn't have much money, and as he passed one of the village bars before he got to the store he went in and spent it, sitting glum and alone with three days' growth of beard on his face. When he found that his money was gone he decided to go to the stream after dark and get some fish. If there was anybody camping they'd be asleep by the time he got there, and he wouldn't use dynamite; the gig would do well enough and if he got a good mess of fish he could always sell some of them to a motel where they didn't question where the fish came from.

He cadged part of a jar of pickled pigs' feet from the bartender, who was glad to get rid of him now that his money was gone, and started home. The jar had been opened for a while and the pigs' feet didn't taste very good, but he gnawed on them as he walked. At the shack he lay down until he thought it was late enough to get moving again. He didn't feel much like going out and cursed the necessity for it, but he finally got his flashlight, gig, and an old potato bag together, pulled on his half-boots, and started out through the woods to reach the stream near Lower Falls where he knew the members seldom came. The members, he thought, were fools; there were fish there and he'd always done pretty well with them.

The moon was nearly full, and if he'd been sober enough to act with his usual craftiness he'd have turned back; but it had been a bad day and the whiskey he'd downed on an empty stomach hadn't helped it. He still wasn't breathing right, he had a bellyache, and he stumbled several times on the rocks in the deeply shadowed path that usually gave him no trouble.

When he reached First Pool he stood on the bank for a moment and shone the flashlight on the water. He could see several trout and a number of suckers, and he dropped the potato bag and began to climb down the bank. It was rocky there, and he stepped on the wrong rock; it rolled beneath his foot and he fell, hitting his head on another rock. Half stunned, he rolled into the pool and thrashed around until his heart stopped. His half-boots filled with water, holding him upright, and he began to float slowly around the pool.

As it happened, he hadn't been alone on the stream. Two of the members, who had come up in separate cars, had dumped their camping gear by arrangement near Fifth Pool without seeing each other, and had fished until dark on different parts of the stream, were together now. They had finished their supper of trout, laid out their air mattresses and sleeping bags, and were sitting contentedly by their fire with their backs against trees. One of them, Julian Strong, was an obstetrician; the other, George Rothiker, was a lawyer. They were both in their fifties and lived near each other on Philadelphia's Main Line; they came to the tract together five or six times during the trout season, when they could both get away during the week, and usually camped overnight.

They had been silent for a time, looking into the fire and puffing on their pipes; presently the moon cleared the ridge to the east, laying small, scattered patches of silvery light in the woods, and Rothiker knocked out his pipe, looked around, and took a deep breath. "Better than the delivery room, isn't it?" he asked.

"There's no money in it," Strong said, and grinned.

"You avaricious quack. You're a credit to the medical-economics course they gave you in medical school. Or you would be, if you didn't waste so much time here."

"I wish I could waste more, while it's still around," Strong said, and lost his grin. "I've picked up a hint of a pipeline coming through."

Rothiker's jaw dropped a little, and he stared at Strong in dismay. "Good Lord," he said. "When did you hear this, Julian?"

"I just heard it yesterday and was going to call Alec, and then an emergency case came up and another one on top of that, and by the time I was finished, it was too late to call him."

"But what . . . How serious is it? I mean, is it set, is it imminent?"

"I don't know much about it," Strong said. "You know how secretive they are about these damned pipelines, for nobody wants one across his place. You can even get a tax deduction for it; your land's considered to be of less value with a pipeline across it."

"But how did you hear about it?"

"I picked it up by chance," Strong said. "I have a patient whose husband is with one of the oil companies and I don't think she realized she'd let it out. She only half implied it, for that matter, and when I got in a careful question or two she clammed up quick. Maybe I'm too jumpy about things like that. I may be making a lot more of it than there is there."

"I know some oil-company lawyers," Rothiker said. "What company is he with?"

"Universal Fuel and Pipeline Corporation."

"I'll see what I can find out, or do about it. It's usually almost impossible to do anything, for they have the right of eminent domain, but I'll get to work on it."

"I'll call Alec tomorrow," Strong said. "Maybe he can get in a lick or two."

They both fell silent again, but this time it was a different silence; the enjoyment and contentment had gone out of it. They were both picturing in their minds the swathe cut through the tract, the trees down and the raw earth eroding into the stream, the great scar across the tract's face that would take years to erase. And the stream itself: what would they do to it, how would the pipeline cross it, and what would the effects be? While there was much soothing talk from the people connected with pipelines, the fact remained that pipelines sometimes leaked or blew up with calamitous effect.

"I guess it's the gas lines that blow up, isn't it?" Rothiker asked. "Is this gas or oil?"

"Oil. I doubt it would blow up. What concerns me is what it would do to the place, or if there was a leak."

"Yes," Rothiker said. That's what he was thinking about, too, and thinking about it brought into his mind the things that had already happened to them, the spraying and the new road and the development that would follow it; as he had driven from the village to the gate, he had seen that trees were being taken down on the line of the new road. He was so disturbed by all this, by the accumulating changes and the possibility of more to come, that he stood up and said: "This gives me ants in the pants, Julian. I think I'll take a stroll before I get into the sack. Want to go along?"

"I think not. I'll stay here and try to condition myself to roll with the punch. Go ahead and walk it off, you'll sleep better. I've had a little more time than you to curse about it."

"Okay," Rothiker said, and started off to walk down the road.

The trees hung over it, and it was more open than the woods and received more moonlight. As he walked through the alternate patches of moonlight and shadow, looking off on either side into the dim, mysterious, tranquil aisles of the forest that harbored so much invisible life which was necessary to its well-being, Rothiker tried to compose himself, to accept the fact that the accelerating change that was overtaking them was inevitable and had to be adjusted to—but there was a question that wouldn't be dismissed: why? Did even this place have to be manipulated and changed for the worse? The tract was so small, tucked away in a corner of the forest, and was held in such affection by those who found pleasure and spiritual satisfaction in it; why couldn't it be let alone? Did a man have to give up something he held precious for what was termed "the common good"—which usually meant profit for someone else? Putting that aside, leaving themselves out of it and taking a larger view, didn't improve the situation; it was another case of a natural area being changed and degraded. Admittedly it was a small area, but it was a microcosm of what was happening in America, which was befouling its rivers and lakes, polluting its air, and seemingly trying to poison itself. All this could be alleviated or controlled with money and thought, but the money and thought always seemed to be spent for a shorter and often dubious gain. Technology, which had given man a start toward mastering nature, was now mastering him.

As a lawyer, Rothiker was all too familiar with the semantics of special pleading; he knew that if it came to a court case, in which they would try to protect themselves, they would stand little chance against the right of eminent domain. They would be a selfish little group trying to withhold benefits from a great number of deserving people . . . who had become a great number by heedlessly overreproducing themselves. Whether the great number of deserving people could be served equally well if the pipeline was moved several miles away would hardly enter the question. And if it did, there would be someone there too who didn't want it and who would perhaps have better political connections than they did.

Rothiker was more naïve, or more idealistic, than his friend Julian; he wasn't quite so ready to curse what was called "progress" and prepare to "roll with the punch." The beauty they had was so much more than the fun of catching fish that he was willing to go to great lengths to preserve it: who knew how badly it would be needed in the future, by many more people than themselves? The pipeline alone would hurt the place but not, if everything went well, ruin it—trees would eventually grow again, the scar would be healed—but, like the new road and the spraying, it was a bite out of the whole, and bite by bite the whole would be eaten up.

In the gloomy frame of mind that held him at the moment Rothiker wasn't optimistic about being able to do much; he could only hope that Julian was wrong or had heard the rumor incorrectly. He hadn't paid much attention to Julian's half disclaimer, being too shocked at the time, but now it came back to him again and hope gave it substance. He began to feel better and get out of himself, to look around with more attention. He was just walking out onto the bridge, and stopped when he got to the middle of it, leaned upon the rail, and looked up and down the stream. The song of the hurrying water was in his ears and he smelled the cool water smell; moonlight glowed silver on the white water spilling over the rock dam of Third Pool above him; Bridge Pool, below him, was more open, and he could see a bat flitting in and out of shadow above it. A fish jumped, leaving widening silvery rings on the water, and a Luna moth flew past him on its way downstream. He could see it for a time, a fluttering little ghost in the moonlight, but he lost it in the shadows near shore over Bridge Pool; perhaps the bat had caught it on its way to a mate. He had heard that a male Luna could scent a female a mile or two away.

As the night, the moth hiding its delicate and lovely colors in the darkness, the leaping fish, and the dark, erratic flight of the bat worked their magic on him he grew more calm and began to feel again the sense of pleasure that the day and all other days on the stream had given him. Julian had been right in sending him off by himself, and now he could go back, but he decided that he wouldn't just yet; he would walk on farther down the stream. He went on across the bridge and left the road to take the path that followed the water. It was darker under the trees but the moonlight came through in places and the path was well worn and not hard to follow.

Feeling like an explorer in a strange and fascinating land, he was careful not to stumble or make any noise, expecting an adventure at every turning of the path. The chorus of the stream's many voices covered his footsteps and any furtive stirrings near at hand, but at a turning near the island he came upon a doe and two fawns in the path. They all stopped; not more than thirty-five feet separated them, and the doe stood with her head up and her ears cocked. She took an uncertain step toward him, stopped again, and stamped a forefoot. She and the fawns beside her were pretty things, and to keep them there he was very still. Finally she decided to go, snorted, and swung about; three raised white tails bounded off into the gloom.

Pleased by the encounter, he went on, pausing for a time beside Lower Falls to listen to the soft roar of the water and watch the moonlight's cold sparkle on the flying drops, and decided to go on to First Pool before turning back. It was a beautiful pool, long and deep and calm on the surface, and he hadn't seen it for a long time; it was really pretty silly that they didn't fish it. He passed Lower Falls Pool and came out at the head of First Pool, screened by brush from the pool at first until a turn in the path brought him out about a third of the way along its length.

His eye was caught by a wandering, diffused spot of light in the water and he stopped, nonplused by such a strange thing. He had never seen its like before and couldn't imagine what it was. He took a step or two to get closer to it, thinking that it might be an unusual effect of the moonlight, and then could vaguely make out a dark thing apparently floating about in the pool, slowly turning and shadowed by the trees.

"What the devil . . . ?" he said aloud, and moved up to the bank.

The thing drifted closer to him, moving slowly out of shadow. It was a man, hunched but more or less upright, with his head over on one shoulder; the moonlight gleamed on one side of his pale face. Rothiker's hair stood up on his head, and he stepped back so hastily that he almost fell.

The shock of his discovery confused him for a long moment, and then he began to make sense. No doubt it was the poacher, Slattery, whom they all knew victimized them occasionally; they all had found a blown can or two along the stream at one time or another. Was he dead? He must be, not to have turned off the flashlight. Rothiker went back to the stream and called: "Hey! Hey!"

The man didn't answer but continued his slow, aimless drifting in and out of shadow. Looking at him more coolly, Rothiker was sure now that there was no life in him. What to do next? He had never had any experience with so-called violent death. Should he pull the corpse out and return to Julian to drive out and get the police, or should he leave it there and let the police cope with it? He decided that Julian, being a doctor, would know more about the procedure than he did and, turning away, started rapidly back to their camp. Julian, who sometimes pretended a cynicism which he didn't feel, would probably remark that it was damned good riddance, and decide what to do.

THREE

JEWELWEED BLOSSOMED and blackberries were ripe; dark purple clusters of elderberries hung in sunny places and partridge berries glowed red among the mosses on the ground. Climbing wild grapes with their small fruit and big fox grapes trailing over old fallen stone fences perfumed the air, and seeds of the summer's growing were everywhere. Squirrels were cutting beechnuts and acorns and pine cones, dropping them down to gather and hide away for winter, and the groundhogs were laying on fat for the long sleep to come.

The first faint intimation of change, of a pause in the strong thrust toward the life-giving sun, could be felt in the shadowy warmth of the forest; there was an almost listless fullness in the millions of leaves, which had almost run their course and presently would flame in the colors of death and drop down, nourishing in their decay to humus the forest floor that fed the roots of the trees that had grown them. The innumerable company of their insect friends and foes, older and more adaptable than man, blindly following the instinct that preserved them, were preparing for another generation in another spring. Katydids were mating, to lay eggs that would overwinter and hatch out wingless young that would hungrily seek out plant lice to devour and grow. May beetles, after passing three years underground as white grubs eating the roots of plants, would emerge and then bury themselves to emerge again in April to mate and lay eggs. The pyrgota fly, smaller than a period on this page, would be watching for them, waiting until they opened their hard wing covers and flew and then swooping down to their unprotected backs to thrust in an egg that would hatch as a larvae and devour its host. The season's final generation of that far traveler, the monarch butterfly, would leave for Canada, remain there until the chill of fall, and then band together and fly to the warm lands of the south. The dark mourning cloaks, first out in the spring, would soon hunt for tree hollows in which to hibernate over the winter, and Isabella tiger-moth caterpillars, "Woolly Bears," were wandering widely to find good places to curl up until spring.

Many insects would hatch as larvae and go into the pupal stages, in which their larval cells would die and slowly be rebuilt over the winter into new organs for a flying life; in the spring they would be reborn with wings. The larvae of the king hornets, "cicada killers," having hatched from eggs and eaten the paralyzed cicadas left in burrows with them, had spun or were spinning cocoons in which to rest over the winter. They would transform into pupae in the spring and dig their way out. Bald-faced hornets and yellow jack-ets, of which all but the queens would die, had a little time yet in their elaborate paper cities before the gathering chill of fall would kill them.

The stream was lower, as it usually was toward the end of sum-mer. This summer had been a rather dry one, and between that and the construction work on the dam in the state park above the tract, the water's level was below that of most years. Many trout, unwill-ing to give up their usual stations, lay in shallow pools between the rocks with their backs almost out of water, alert and quick to rush off to cracks in the stream-side ledges. Fishermen found them diffi-cult to approach and thought there were fewer of them, and often stumbled upon them and frightened them off. They were harder to catch in any event after the summer's feeding and the concentration of stream life caused by low water. They were lazy and fat; but in the fat, concentrated little by little first from the flying insects killed by the spraying and later by worms and stream life which had themselves concentrated it from the earth and the run-off from the surrounding forest, lay the possibility of death when winter came and they drew on the fat for sustenance. There had been a high mortality among the eggs of the rainbow trout; the hatch had been very small.

The old trout in S Pool, which had taken Ohlmstead's bait and then eluded him, spent a good many of the daylight hours in his dark labyrinth beneath the ledge. Since his narrow escape from dis-aster he had been warier than ever, for as the weather warmed and the stream fell, slowing the wild rush of current through the pool, more fishermen had tried one way or another to fish it and some had brought their children to swim or paddle about in it. Ohlmstead had tried several times to catch him without success, and had finally decided to give him up for the season and make a well-planned descent upon him early next spring, when he would be hungry and forgetful.

"Enough people are throwing all sorts of junk at him now," he said to Mrs. McIntyre, his housekeeper, whom he had told of his involuntary swim, swearing her to secrecy, "and he doesn't look at it. He's got the longest memory of any trout I ever saw, and they're just reminding him to keep on using it. But in the spring . . . when the young man's fancy turns to thoughts of love, mine will turn toward him. I'll get him yet."

"It would be a nice feather in your cap," she said, "to catch him and show him to the others, and them not even knowing he's there."

"It would, indeed," he said. "Besides that, he's been there long enough, and probably runs every other trout out of that pool. Nobody's caught much in it."

He was pretty nearly right, for the old trout had become more of a tyrant; he wanted the pool to himself, had driven out the others which shared it with him, and attacked savagely any other fish that came into it. He had become morose, for the spray that had been accumulating in his body was beginning to affect his nervous system, the tensions of the breeding season were building up in him, and Ohlmstead's hook was still in his jaw. In itself it was a small thing, but the several feet of monofilament (which sometimes caught in the cracks in the rocks, until it broke off short) had frightened and irritated him and he had rubbed his jaw on rocks to get rid of it until some of his skin had worn off and water mold, fungus, had attacked these spots. They were covered with a fuzzy pale growth that, now it had a foothold, would spread and work inward and at long last consume him, more quickly because his vitality was down. Ohlmstead, who plotted his downfall, had contributed to it without knowing it.

The young raccoons from the old tree at the edge of Bear Swamp had grown a good deal and were now out with their parents, and their curiosity about the world was inexhaustible. There were four of them, and their mother was hard put to it to keep an eye on them all. For a time after their first descent from the tree they followed her closely but now they were growing more independent, making little excursions of their own, climbing about in the trees, poking their sharp little muzzles and pawlike hands into everything, tasting everything, and leaving no stone unturned in their explorations. They were much like little monkeys in their endless pryings.

In their family expeditions along the stream and the spring runs in the darkness of the night they didn't always return to the old tree; sometimes they were too far from it when the sky began to pale, and slept away the day in old hawk or owl nests or tree hollows that the old male had found in his wanderings. Sometimes they took sunbaths together, sprawled on limbs above the greenery below, invisible from the ground. The young ones fought sham battles, puffing themselves up and scuttling crabwise upon each other, occasionally losing their tempers and falling into screeching fights which the old ones broke up. It was a good time for them. There was plenty to eat and not too much work to find it. Berries and grapes were ripe, what crawfish and frogs were about were easier to get at with the water low, and fish lying in the shallow little pools left by the falling water could often be caught. They learned that toads were not frogs but had poison in their skins, and that some insects which had fire in their tails by day were safe to approach by night. There were few troubles, for the horned owls which might have picked off a straying young one or two before they got too big had moved and they had no other enemies that would care to face the disastrous fighting ability of the old raccoons.

The prospect of all of them surviving the winter comfortably together in the old beech was good until the night they came upon the camp of a member named Houston, near Hemlock Pool. Houston, a rather new member camping out for the first time, had been there for two days, but late that afternoon his pointer, whom he had brought along for a run in the woods while he fished, had caught the young porcupine and killed it, getting a face and mouth full of quills. Houston had taken the dog to a vet eighteen miles away and had had to wait several hours for the vet to get home. His camp was deserted when the raccoons found it.

The scents of man and dog were strong, but so were the more enticing ones of things to eat. The raccoons were on the other side of the stream and the old ones were at first inclined to avoid the camp by a wide and hasty detour, but after listening for a time and hearing no sounds they succumbed to temptation. The young ones wanted to explore this new thing and were difficult to restrain, and finally the old male led them all across the stream on rocks that stood above the water, and made a cautious approach. As Houston had been getting ready for dinner when the dog came in full of quills and they had left hurriedly, nothing had been put away. There was a steak in the frying pan; and bread, butter, and lettuce, and several tomatoes in a plate on top of the refrigerator box. This windfall received attention first. Houston hadn't latched the box, and it gave off more fine scents; the lid was soon opened, and the box's contents followed the other food. By this time the young raccoons' bellies were bulging and they had lost their interest in eating, but their curiosity was as lively as ever and they moved on Houston's little tent.

Two of them circled it several times, churring to themselves and trying to get in; one of the others, seeing the interior through the mosquito netting at the door, chewed a hole in the netting and opened the way. Soon they were all inside. One found a bar of chocolate and took it into a corner; two found Houston's open tackle box and fished everything out of it, making rat's nests of tapered lines and leaders. The fourth one got into the sleeping bag, was puzzled by the soft feel of its down filling, chewed a hole in it, and pulled down out by the handful.

The old male came in and after a moment froze to a listening attitude. He had caught a sound and concentrated on it; it was Houston coming back up the rocky path from his car at the end of the road near Eighth Pool, and the old raccoon, urgently calling the young to follow him, ran out through the rent in the netting. Three of them did, but the one in the sleeping bag became confused and went down further into it, entangled himself, and was trapped.

Houston didn't have the dog with him; they had had to anesthetize it, and he would get it the next day. He came into his camp and the flashlight showed him the havoc that had been wrought with his refrigerator box and his dinner. He ran to the tent, unzipped the mosquito netting, and went inside. The white scattered down was the first thing he saw, and he turned the light on the bag. The young raccoon was fighting desperately inside it, and the bag was heaving and rolling about as though possessed by an evil spirit. Houston fell back in dismay, then ran out, picked up the frying pan, and ran back and beat the thing in the bag until it moved no more.

He was shaking when he finished beating the bag, and went outside, threw some wood on the embers of his fire, and sat down for a time to calm himself. Presently he went into the tent again and brought his bag out, dumped the raccoon and the puffs of down out of it, and assayed the damage. He was cleaned out of food and had little taste for getting into the bloody, ripped-up bag. He cursed wholeheartedly and decided to go back to the village again. Ohlmstead would put him up for the night, or else he'd find a meal and a bed somewhere else.

Ohlmstead didn't fish much this late in the summer except for a little work with a small dry fly and a long fine leader early in the morning or toward dusk, for the weather was warm, the water was low, and the trout rather indifferent, but he still spent a good deal of time along the stream. He felt about it the way garden lovers feel about their gardens; to be near it gave him a feeling of serenity and pleasure, and he could be happy just sitting at some point of vantage to watch the tumbling water and the quiet woods around it. Birds moved around him; chipmunks, red and gray squirrels went about their concerns; and occasionally he saw larger game that remained unaware of him. At these times he got out of himself and felt he was truly a part of the natural world, not an alien who had invaded it to do in some creature and carry its carcass home.

This side of his nature, which he kept to himself, would have astonished his friends, who looked upon him as a keen and dedicated hunter and fisherman. Sometimes it rather puzzled him, as when he had a good shot at a woodcock or a grouse and stood watching it fly off, forgetting his gun in the pleasure of seeing the creature dodge off through the openings in the bright autumn woods. After the bird had vanished he would remember the gun, look at it, shake his head, and shoot at the next bird. When he tried to explain this to himself he got nowhere; it was too paradoxical and involved for him.

Several days after he had put Houston up for the night he was sitting beside S Pool and ordinarily would have fallen into one of these moods, but this day he was too disturbed to manage it. As he had driven from the village he had seen bulldozers for the first time at work on the new road; he had hoped that they wouldn't get at it until next year, that there would be a little more time before another evidence of progress and encirclement appeared, but now he saw that the hope had been a vain one. He was sure that the banks of the road wouldn't be seeded until the following spring, and if there were bad storms there would be erosion. Thinking of that brought him to the pipeline and further disturbed him. The members still knew little one way or the other, for neither Rothiker nor Alec Goodenow had been able to find out anything more, and the prospects remained as troubling as a storm over the horizon.

Having got into these gloomy thoughts, he had more. He hadn't seen as many young grouse as usual as he wandered about on the tract; the several broods he had seen—including the first one, from which he had taken the drowned chick to hook the old trout—had been very small. Usually there were a dozen young or so, at least for a time, but this year there seemed to be half a dozen young or less, and he wondered if the spring spraying was responsible for that. It was hard to tell with grouse; they were cyclical in their abundance, the grouse population went up and down, but the reports he'd had from other parts of the state didn't indicate a decline. There didn't seem to be as many woodcock either, and as he thought back on it, comparing the bird life on the tract with his recollections of other years, it seemed to him that the populations of other species were smaller, too.

He had finally heard from his friend, the research biologist. Photostats of several scientific papers had come with the letter, and while they were rather technical, embodying a great deal of experimental data and procedure, they confirmed what he had already gathered in a general way: the chlorinated hydrocarbons persisted for years; they either lay in the soil to be eaten by insects and worms or washed into streams to be eaten by life forms there. Birds, animals, and fish that ate these creatures accumulated the insecticide in their fat, and when their bodies called on the fat in winter the accumulated poison was released and damaged or killed them. Further, calcium metabolism in nesting birds was disturbed, resulting in eggshells that broke because they were too thin, or embryos that died before they hatched. The effect on trout was bad, too; when the fry hatched they carried egg sacs to nourish them for a time, and the hydrocarbons that their mothers had built up from the poisoned insects they had eaten were passed on in the fat of the egg sacs, to be absorbed by the fry.

These insecticides were in the water, on the land, and in the air over most of the earth now, even in places far from where they had been used, and everything that ate it, from the plankton in a "safe" concentration to the fish that ate the plankton to the birds or beasts that ate them again all concentrated it more and more until at the

131

top of the food chain the concentration might have increased ten million times. Predators at the top of their food chains, such as bald eagles, peregrine falcons, ospreys, brown pelicans, cormorants, and mergansers, were vanishing, indeed had vanished, from many parts of their old ranges.

"So," the letter ended, "there you are. Some people think that the process of photosynthesis, which comes up with about 70% of the earth's oxygen, will eventually be hindered. We're waking up; the Feds are moving against DDT, but not much has been done about the others—aldrin, dieldrin, hexachlor, and so on—yet. These things have done a lot of good in their time, and while over a hundred insects once controlled are now immune to them, they are still very effective control agents."

What all this was doing to them Ohlmstead had no way of knowing, but it scared him; what had started out as a great boon to mankind seemed to be turning into a disaster as many other things were doing, and where were the boundaries of the calamities it could bring? They didn't have the troubles of the river—raw sewage, garbage, steel-mill acids, mine drainage, heat pollution from power plants, and God knew how many other chemical wastes— but things were changing and their turn might come any day. A few years ago their most vexing problem was a simple poacher, but now . . .

Thinking of the poacher, and the night Rothiker and Strong had got him out of bed to help them find the local constable and legally dispose of Slattery's corpse, Ohlmstead was sidetracked from his glum meditations and had to grin. Rothiker had been shocked, Strong cynically grateful for fate's disposition of Slattery, and the constable—after solemnly talking about inquests, courts of inquiry, and whatnot—had been calmed down and shown the simple way to settle the affair. He, Ohlmstead, hadn't got back to bed until nearly dawn, but thinking of the affair now he recalled how beautiful First Pool had been in the moonlight after they had got Slattery and his flashlight out of it, and suddenly decided that he would feel better if he went and looked at it again. He got up and walked back to his car, drove down the road until he was above First Pool, and started down the hill through the woods.

At the bottom of the hill there was a little floodplain on the western side of the stream; trees and brush were thick there, and before Ohlmstead got through them he heard voices—a man's and a woman's. There were plenty of no-trespassing signs on the trees here and between here and the highway, and Ohlmstead decided that before he walked up to the people he would slow down and make a detour to see who they were and what they were up to.

He came out above the falls and was well concealed in the brush. They were below the falls, on the bank, naked and lying side by side; what they had been up to was fairly evident by their postures of contented relaxation. Ohlmstead watched them for a moment, feeling a little envy of their youth and their pleasure in each other, and then grinned. He thought they were probably honeymooners from the Seneca, a large summer hotel a few miles up the highway.

The girl sat up, leaned over to kiss the man, and got to her feet. She had dark hair and a beautiful figure, with splendid, high breasts; she stood there for a moment, smiling down at the man, dappled with sunlight and shadow, and said: "Come on, Don. Let's swim."

The man stood up, reached down for a can of beer, drained it, and threw it along with three others into the stream before he helped her down the high steep bank and into the water.

Ohlmstead had half turned away, but the cans thrown into the stream pulled him up. The gesture, so typical of our time, of people cluttering the land with trash and the air and water with destructive chemicals and God knew what else because it cost a little more money or effort to dispose of satisfactorily, suddenly made him furious because it seemed so universal and almost impossible to cope with. His first impulse was to deal directly with this particular man, to move out of cover and make him pick up the cans and leave, but then he remembered the girl and their nakedness. He couldn't do it; there was a sort of delicacy in him, a modesty that was rather old-fashioned but unyielding that made it impossible. Stumped, he let his streak of whimsicality take hold as it had in his dealings with the old trout in Upper Falls Pool. Moving silently and swiftly, he reached the place where the man and woman had been, gathered up their clothes, and climbed the hill. Halfway up, he thrust the clothes under a rotted log, hid them in among dead leaves, got into his car, and drove home.

Ohlmstead was reading the paper after lunch the next day when Mrs. McIntyre came in. She was a little earlier than usual and by her expression it was evident that she had tidings, probably scandalous, that she couldn't bear to keep to herself.

"You certainly look full of news," Ohlmstead said. "Who's been caught with his fingers in somebody else's till this morning?"

"The things that go on," she said. "I declare."

"Ah," Ohlmstead said, putting down the paper.

"You wouldn't believe it. You just wouldn't believe it."

She shook her head and raised her eyes to the ceiling. Ohlmstead grinned, for there were always these preliminaries to build suspense, and he played along with them. He leaned forward, and said: "Tell me."

"Well. My John got called from the Seneca last night. One of the commodes got stopped up, or something, and their man wasn't there. There was a lot of water running, and they were afraid it would come through the floor, or the ceiling. It was on the second floor."

"I see."

"It was after dark, too. It was almost bedtime, and my John was looking at a basketball game on TV. You know how he hates to leave a basketball game."

"Do I not?" Ohlmstead said.

"Well, he went. He got his plunger and the snake and his wrenches and went. Mumbling to himself."

Ohlmstead nodded.

"When he got up near your creek, a little past it . . . Oh, my. What do you think he saw?"

"A bear," Ohlmstead said, with a straight face.

"A bear? A bare man. He was bare, but he had ferns and leaves on. Did you ever?"

"He was standing in the road?" Ohlmstead asked. "Go on, go on."

"He sort of came out of the bushes and held up his hand. My John didn't know whether to stop or not, you know how people get held up, but he did stop, and this man . . . he was embarrassed like, asked my John if he'd take them . . . Them, mind you, to the Seneca. He said they were swimming and somebody stole their clothes. He said he'd pay my John ten dollars to take them in the back way to their cabin. My John said he reckoned he could, and then this girl came running out of the bushes in leaves and ferns too and jumped in the back seat. My John said it was like the Garden of Eden."

Ohlmstead was laughing heartily, but he managed a hopeful question: "Could he see whether there was any poison ivy among the leaves?"

"He said he didn't look. He said. And then the man introduced her as his wife." Mrs. McIntyre paused and with a sudden sarcastic look added: "H'm. I'll bet. Playing like Adam and Eve in your creek with a man, and then running around in front of my John with a few leaves on. If they stayed on." She shook her head. "My John didn't sleep so good, either, he was tossing and turning most of the night. Well, summer people . . ."

"John was probably laughing to himself and didn't want to wake you."

"Well, I hope so. Well, I got to get the upstairs done," she said, and went off. Bringing John and his Garden of Eden into the story had clouded her pleasure in it.

Left to himself, Ohlmstead chuckled for a time, and then nodded his head. He'd fixed the beer-can thrower, he thought; it was one of his finest hours in the cause of conservation and a cleaner world. He chuckled again, this time at himself in irony because he had done so little in a cause that concerned him so much. But in the things that had happened to them, what more could he have done?

AUTUMN

ONE

HE AIR was lighter now, with a cool bright clarity that had not been there when the warmth of summer lay somnolently beneath the trees, and in the mornings the ridge beyond the river to the east was softened by autumn haze. After the coolness of dawn there was a drowsiness about the days that was different from the drowsiness of summer, for now the growing was over and the fruits of the growing were ripe; the world of green things rested and began to prepare for the long still time of winter sleep.

Some of the birds of summer had gone, and new ones from the north appeared. Great flocks of blackbirds, noisy and restless, slid through the trees and gathered in gleaming companies on the ground for a day or two; waves of robins followed them. More quietly, as though in secret because they migrated at night, the warblers began to come through in mixed flocks. Early morning saw them dropping in, but resting or feeding they weren't very noticeable, hidden in the hemlocks, in laurel thickets, or high in the oaks, glimpsed and gone. A small flock of black-crowned night heron roosted for a day in a dead oak near Twelfth Pool, and an old great blue heron, driven from the river by a boy with a .22 rifle, found the stream after they had gone and spent several days along the western bank of S Pool, where the shore sloped down gradually to deep, fast water. A dignified and picturesque bird, he stood knee-deep in the stream, motionless as a stone for long periods until some unwary water-dweller moved within range; then his snaky neck and rapier beak would dart out and stab it and he would toss it into the air and swallow it head-first. Everything that moved, as well as fish, was grist for his mill: snakes, insects, frogs, or mice. In their season young birds were eaten too. Trout streams weren't his usual hunting ground, but for a short time he found this one secure and quiet enough to suit him.

After he left for the south, lifting off with his great seventy-inch wings, the signs of fall increased. Sumac berries were red and the leaves were turning, dogwood scattered through the forest gradually took on the crimson of autumn; the vermilion of Virginia creeper splashed color on the tumble-down lichened gray stone walls of an earlier day. A few milkweed pods were opening to set their winged seeds adrift on the breeze, and walnuts were falling. As the blaze of color deepened and spread, tulip trees and hickories glowed golden, maples blazed in crimson and gold, beeches and oaks wore bronze; the unchanging hemlocks gave dark contrast to them all. Until the wind moved them away, bright leaves rested

lightly on the rocks of the stream, or gathered in the eddies. The melancholy of summer's dying was lost in splendor.

Drones and new queens of the yellow jackets and bald-faced hornets, produced late in the summer to save food, had mated; drones that had fertilized the queens had died and the queens had gone off to hibernate. The old cities, with their expanding and elaborate brood combs, galleries, and insulating air spaces, once humming with busy thousands, would fall to ruins as the workers wandered off to die or stayed to eat the larvae they had so carefully tended and wait for the cold to kill them.

Mantises, grown to five or six inches, were mating and laying their eggs in frothy cases that would harden to overwinter; females often voraciously ate their mates as the mating proceeded. Many of the woolly-bear caterpillars that were hurrying about to find good places to hibernate would be caught by skunks, who would roll them over and over with their paws to remove the hairs. More and more insects were dying as the autumn nights grew cooler; fewer spider webs glittered with cold dew in the mornings, club mosses sent out their clouds of spores when some creature's passing shook them, and many fungi appeared, coming to fruition on rotting logs or thrusting up through the leaves of the forest floor.

There was food everywhere to fatten the creatures which had to survive the hungry time of winter. Deer, grouse, raccoons, and squirrels gorged on acorns; squirrels and chipmunks and mice stored acorns and beechnuts and seeds. The forest, bogs, and distant fields held enough for them all, the ones which would stay and the waves of migrants pausing as they moved along their ancient and mysterious routes to the south. There was a great going and coming beneath the brilliant canopy of leaves.

The male woodcock which had returned to the tract in the spring and the female with which he had mated had both survived the summer and raised a single chick. There had been four eggs and three of them had failed to hatch, for the eggshells had been too fragile. The fourth one had just managed to get out into the world and his life had been nearly ended soon after, for a raccoon had come upon the nest. Just before he pounced upon it, the mother, seeing that it wouldn't escape the thief, had taken the young bird between her thighs and flown off with him to a safe place.

It had been touch and go with him for a time in the new location, for the insecticide bequeathed to him by his mother had weakened him. He had finally gained strength and grown up, though, and the little family had drifted apart. They frequently encountered one another at their feeding stations but spent their days in different places. The old male clung to the tangle above the swamp; his mate found a place to her liking on higher ground near Hemlock Pool; and the young bird spent his days near the quaking bog on the ridge. They were well scattered by day, each in his dry, protected place, to doze away the bright hours. No man had troubled them all spring and summer, but now this was changed; the grouse and woodcock season opened.

The night before the opening, Houston came up from Philadelphia with his pointer and stayed with Ohlmstead; the next morning they were on the tract before the dew was quite dry on the brush. It was a sunny, cool morning with a high and cloudless sky, a perfect autumn day in which it was a delight to be alive, and the two men grinned at each other when they got out of Ohlmstead's station wagon and loaded their guns above Lower Falls. Ohlmstead had suggested that they stop here and walk down the hill, for he had often found a grouse in the thicket on the western side of the stream.

"Maybe there'll be one there today," he said. "Then we can cross and work our way up, cross back around Upper Falls, and work back the other side. If that old woodcock above Fifth Pool is still around, we ought to find him; I don't know whether there are any across the stream or not. How are you on woodcock?" he asked, because he'd never shot with Houston. He liked Houston but didn't know how experienced Houston was; he was going to stay behind him until he saw how he handled a gun, for he suspected, after Houston's fiasco with the young raccoon in the sleeping bag, that he had a few things to learn.

"I could be better," Houston said. "I've hunted them for two years, but I still have to knock one down. The dog's better than I am. A friend of mine who owned him died, and his widow gave him to me just before the season opened last year. If you have any suggestions I'd admire to hear them, for last year we got up quite a few birds in the Alleghenies and I missed them all. The dog began looking at me as though he thought I was wasting his time." He grinned.

This was modestly said and pleased Ohlmstead, for he had been of two minds when Houston suggested they open the season together. He liked a shooting companion occasionally, and the other members who shot lived near each other and usually came up in pairs; if Houston turned out to suit him they could have some enjoyable times together. "Let's go down the hill," he said, and they started off.

He had shot over some good dogs and had owned several of his own, and he was pleased to see that this one started off as though it knew its business; it ranged well but not too widely and kept an eye on the hunters. Halfway down the hill it jumped a log, stopped, swung about, and pawed under the log to reveal the bathers' clothes that Ohlmstead had hidden. It stood looking at them, wagging its tail.

Houston stared at the clothes. "What do you think happened here?" he asked, a little perturbed. "Do you think there's been a murder on the place?" He moved a bit closer. "There's a woman's outfit here too."

"That's right," Ohlmstead said. "Damned pretty woman she was, too."

Houston looked at him questioningly. "You know about this? Is it something . . . I mean, if there's something I ought to know about . . . Well, hell, I don't know what I mean."

"Maybe you mean, has the club a guilty secret. Not the club. Me." He told Houston about the bathers, and what Mrs. McIntyre had told him.

Houston laughed so heartily that he had to sit down on the log; the dog came up, laid its head in his lap, and rolled up its eyes at him. "By Judas!" he said finally. "It was in a good cause, but you're a hard man. What a way to let the air out of love's young dream."

"It was a dirty trick," Ohlmstead said, "but love's young dream shouldn't be tossing beer cans into the stream. There are so many things that we can't fix that when one came along that I could express myself about, I did it."

Still chuckling, Houston got off the log and they went on downhill. At the bottom of it, in the brush on the little floodplain, the pointer checked, came to a point, and then began to pussyfoot forward one careful step at a time.

"The bird's here," Ohlmstead said, "and moving. Close up behind the dog. I'll parallel you on the right."

In the excitement of the moment, of waiting tense and ready for the first grouse of the season to flush, Ohlmstead ignored his earlier decision to stay behind Houston for the first shot or two; perhaps he had already assayed the man from what he had said. With his gun held across his chest he moved off to the right and then turned to parallel Houston, who he saw wasn't closing in fast enough, for when a grouse moved ahead of the dog like this one was doing, it was likely to flush out of range unless the man pushed it. He'd have to mention this to Houston, who apparently didn't know quite what to do. He picked up his own pace and then heard the lovely thunder of the bird taking off.

He saw a flash of movement and knew that the grouse was turning to cross the stream; the next instant he saw it fully, tail spread, broadside to him, and climbing steeply—a long, very difficult snap shot as it roared up into an opening through the bright leaves, silhouetted briefly against the pure blue of the sky. It was the quickest of snap shots, with only an instant for his brain to coordinate lead and swing and the pressure of his finger on the trigger, and when the gun went off, the grouse rolled over and came down.

He slowly lowered the gun, filled with exultation and regret. It had been a beautiful shot, and of that he was proud; the regret was that he had brought low a creature that was to him the greatest game bird on earth. He loved the grouse and always had this confused emotion when he shot one, this dichotomy, when the shot brought it down; he had long since given up trying to explain it to himself. The dog came up with the bird in its mouth and sat down before him, wagging its tail in the leaves. He stroked it and said a few words before he took the bird. It was big, the cock from west of S Pool; it had been concentrating on the dog and Houston, and its luck had run out.

"A very handsome shot, from what I could see," Houston said, coming up. "He was a little far for me, and too soon out of sight. When he started to swing toward you I thought I'd better hold my fire."

"You should have moved in faster," Ohlmstead said, relieved that his intuition about Houston had been correct. "A smart character like this one can get too far ahead of you if you don't. And any time you want to sell the pointer, let me know first."

"I promise," Houston said. "You've restored his faith. I'll move faster next time."

"Next time the bird will fly straight at your head, or get behind a tree," Ohlmstead said, putting the grouse in his pocket. "They never do the same thing twice and practically always do the unexpected. They take the best you've got, and that's why I have such an affection for them. Better luck next time."

They crossed the stream on the rocks above Lower Falls and worked their way over higher ground toward the edge of Bear Swamp. There was an area of gray birch near the top of the hill before they dropped down; the leaves were turning and the patch was floored with grass and blackberry vines, and the dog came on point just inside the trees. The old female woodcock had come there instead of to her usual place at dawn, and the dog had found her.

"Woodcock, maybe," Ohlmstead said, "and all yours."

"Aren't you going to shoot?"

"No," Ohlmstead said. "I'll watch you break your jinx. Go ahead." He fell in behind Houston, who moved up toward the dog.

Nothing happened for a long moment. Houston, as though he was walking on eggs, moved around the dog and then in front of it. Still nothing happened, and he turned to look at Ohlmstead in puzzlement. At that moment the woodcock flushed; it came up right beside him, almost climbing his leg, and rose through the trees, twittering. Houston was caught off balance and his flustered shot was behind the bird; as he got off a second hurried shot the woodcock took a swift right-angled turn and he was behind it again. It vanished from view and the dog turned to Ohlmstead and gave him such a look of reproach that he burst out laughing.

"Oh, damn! Damn!" Houston said. "You see how the little devils bug me? Now the dog hates me and I hate myself and I'm about to hate you too." He broke his gun in disgust and reloaded. "Shall we follow him up?"

"I don't usually do it. It wouldn't be too hard to find him again, two or three times maybe, but if I miss 'em I let 'em go until next time. I'll go along if you want, though."

"No, I think you're right. Such a nasty little bird deserves a break, as much as it hurts me. Why do you think I missed him?"

"You lost your concentration," Ohlmstead said. "You didn't flush him right away and were puzzled and looked at me and your mind wandered. Being psychic," he went on with a grin, "the bird knew that, and took a mean advantage of you. And that might not be as silly as it sounds, either. From the number of times that birds flush when you're distracted for one reason or another, you'd think they had some sort of ESP."

"They certainly seem to work it on me."

"That one seemed to. He waited until he knew you didn't believe the dog; this disbelief broke your concentration and threw you out of readiness and he flushed. He caught you flat-footed." They started to walk again. "Hitting a bird moving fast in three dimensions," he went on, "takes great coordination of nerves, muscles, and judgment, a rhythm of these things, and *that* takes concentration; if the concentration is broken the rhythm fails somewhere." He laughed. "The devil! I sound like a stuffy professor belaboring the obvious, but I do love the shotgun. To me it's not an instrument of slaughter but an instrument as demanding and as intricate to manipulate well as a violin. Period. End of speech. Of course you can use it for slaughter, but no decent man would. I'm sure you could also use a violin to drive people out of their minds."

"You may sound stuffy to yourself," Houston said, after walking along silently for several minutes, "but you don't sound stuffy to me. I think maybe I've been too much of a meat hunter, with my mind fixed on knocking something down." He shook his head. "Maybe that's why I beat that poor young raccoon to death. It was a stupid thing to do."

Ohlmstead was pleased at this evidence of progress, and smiled. They felt they knew each other a little better now, and a feeling of deeper companionship descended upon them as they dropped down the hill and came to the edge of Bear Swamp. The dog turned up the spring run and they followed it. On the other side, fifty yards away and downwind a grouse and four young ones that she had raised were feeding and heard them. They froze to listen and remained immobile until the two men were out of hearing. Their time of being together was almost over, for soon an impulse to separate and seek new territories of their own, called by men "the fall shuffle," would enter into them and they would go a little crazy for a time, flying about with more than their usual heedless reckless-ness. At the best of times they were reckless enough, dashing at speed through branches and brush; when this fit was on them they would sometimes fly blindly into trees or other objects and stun or kill themselves.

Moving down from the northern Adirondacks for the winter, the young female goshawk had followed the ancient pathway of mi-grating hawks, eagles, and many other species of birds moving south, crossing southeastern New York a few miles above New York City into Pennsylvania and down the long ridge of Blue Mountain, taking advantage of the winds and updrafts along the ridge. She turned off before reaching the concentration point at Hawk Mountain Sanctuary, where in former years thousands of hawks had been shot in the name of sport, and wandered about until she came to the stream at the northern end of the tract.

She had left the north before her parents and this was her first migration; possibly the urge was already dying out in her and she had turned off to explore. She liked the little valley with its mixed deciduous trees and evergreens and the stream; the nest in which she had been hatched was on a hillside overlooking a stream and a beaver pond, and the tract might have reminded her of it. When she came to the stream she found a little backwater where the water wasn't too deep or swift and took a bath, rolling from side to side and ducking her head until she was very wet before hopping up on a rock to preen herself and dry in a patch of golden sunshine.

Like all her race, she was a secretive bird and spent most of her time in concealment, waiting and watching for prey to come within reach and then making a swift and deadly dash at it. She was rather like a cat in her hunting, patiently waiting an opportunity, fast and extraordinarily maneuverable, able to dash about in the brush and twist and turn like a bat, and when her long curved talons got hold of something it seldom escaped. Her eyes, which rarely missed anything that went on around her, were yellow; they would turn a brilliant fiery red in a year or so, when she had dropped her brown juvenile feathers and assumed the gray of maturity. Young as she was, she was a very efficient predator, for her parents had taught her well and she had been an apt pupil.

When she was dry she flew high into a hemlock but couldn't see well enough from it and changed her perch to a higher branch of a nearby sycamore. Seventy feet above the forest floor she watched two distant chipmunks at their final harvesting for a time, but they were skimpy fare and too much in the open to tempt her. After an hour or so she dropped from the sycamore to within a few feet of the ground and slipped through the woods like a deadly shadow until she came to the bog on the ridge, where she swooped up to take a stand in a maple.

The blueberry bushes spotted through the bog and around its edge, glowing deep red against the unchanging green of Labrador tea, the gray of scattered rocks, and the sphagnum floor of the bog itself, held little of interest to her; she concentrated her attention on the higher ground beneath the encircling trees. Nothing moved for a long time, but at last her patience was rewarded; a rabbit appeared from behind a tree forty yards to the left of her, hopped in a leisurely way across a little opening, and vanished behind another tree.

She dropped from her perch and with the momentum gained

glided low along the bog's edge, whipped around the tree behind which the rabbit had gone, and checked for an instant to locate him. He had gone on a little farther and the sudden flash of wings startled him so that he leaped out instead of freezing, which might have saved him. He tried to stay in cover but the hawk was after him with such an extraordinary burst of speed that she was over him for a few yards, shifting as he dodged. He dashed through a tall and seemingly impenetrable briar thicket, but without checking her speed she picked a small opening, folded her wings and slid through it, and took him in the little clearing on the other side of it. He screamed as one foot caught him by the head and the other by the loin and turned a complete somersault, but his race was over; the hawk's iron grip held him, and when they came to earth again she propped herself with her wings and finished him. It had been a typical goshawk maneuver, executed with great dash and remarkable control.

She took her time to pluck most of the fur from the rabbit and eat him, and then flew back to the hemlocks along the stream and took a perch in their thick cover. The day was waning and the crimson flare of sunset in the western sky scarcely penetrated the gloom of the thicket; she fluffed out her feathers against the evening's chill and prepared to settle down for the night. A grouse on its way to roost walked through the thicket almost immediately below her, but good fortune was with him; her crop full of rabbit, she quietly watched him move out of sight.

The next morning she didn't stir until the sun had been up for a time, waiting until she cast up, in a pellet, the fur and bones of the rabbit she had swallowed with her meat. When that was done, after much gaping and twisting of her neck, she was hungry again and ready for the day. Presently she flew out of the hemlock and up the stream for a way, rising to perch in a tree between the tract's boundary and the spring run above Thirteenth Pool. Clumps of hemlocks grew in this portion of the tract, alternating with oaks under which ferns grew that had now turned brown, and her view was spotty. Nothing moved for an hour, and then her keen ears caught the distant voices of Houston and Ohlmstead and soon after that the sounds of the pointer quartering in the fallen leaves. The men had walked to the boundary, crossed the stream and detoured the stony area of the bear's old den, and were moving downstream toward her.

Their voices didn't mean anything to her, being outside her experience, but her suspicious and secretive nature inclined her to slip away. She was just about to do this when a hen grouse, which had been drifting along well in front of the dog, walked out of a clump of hemlocks not far away. She dropped from her tree at it, and catching the flicker of motion, it spun about and rose in flight toward the men.

They heard the grouse take off without being quite able to locate its position, but they were alerted and ready to shoot if it should come their way. It burst out of the hemlocks in front of Houston, flying at top speed with the goshawk in close pursuit, and went over his head. It was a quick snap shot and Houston took it, but he was so confused by seeing two birds, almost in tandem, instead of one, that his aim was thrown off. One pellet clipped a long outside tail feather off the goshawk close to her body. The roar of the gun and the shock of the pellet made her swerve, and seeking to escape she fled down the stream and off the tract. She would never return to it, and continued toward the south.

The severed tail feather spun slowly down to land almost at Houston's feet. He picked it up and held it out to Ohlmstead. "I'm improving," he said. "I got a feather. I never saw such a thing; it looked like a whole train of birds. Do you know what that second thing was?"

"Everything happened pretty fast," Ohlmstead said, and took the feather, "but it looked like a goshawk from where I stood. From this feather, I'd say that was what it was. They were right over your head and I couldn't shoot, but I think you saved the grouse for another day. It would have been caught, I'm sure, and I hope you convinced the hawk it had better move somewhere else. We'll have more grouse if it does, for it's too damned good at catching them. At the same time, I'm glad you didn't kill it. It has its place, like everything else." He stuck the feather in Houston's hat. "Homeopathic magic," he said. "Now you'll be as good a hunter as the hawk."

"I'm not sure I want to be," Houston said, with an appearance of innocence, as they started off again. "It sounds suspiciously like sophistry to say we should dispossess the hawk because we want the grouse. If nature tries to balance itself, as you say, the grouse belongs more to it than to us, and we're throwing the balance out of whack if we shoot them. I doubt I should be a party to it."

Ohlmstead nodded. "Your scruples do you credit," he said, and added: "Not that you've needed them so far."

"Your case is a little different," Houston said. "You can hit them."

"Oh, my influence is modest," Ohlmstead said blandly. "I take two or three a year, and some of the other members collect a few. Any good wildlife biologist will tell you that a large percentage of the hatch doesn't make it over the winter, so out of this lost percentage we might as well harvest a few. Share them with the foxes, goshawks, and horned owls. They have as much responsibility toward us as we have toward them, for we protect their tract so far as we're able."

"Oh, me," Houston said. "Oh, good heavens. So now you're a benefactor, a—"

"No, you are. You support a dog all year to help you find these creatures in order to balance them, and the dog is on point right now."

He gestured up the hill. Fifty yards away, among the scrub oak and knee-high brush, the dog had found a woodcock from the north that had dropped in toward dawn. He came to a firm and beautiful point.

Houston had shifted his gun to his shoulder, and now he hurriedly brought it to a position of readiness and scrambled up the hill. "Come on," he said over his shoulder. "Let's go."

Ohlmstead smiled and followed him. He stopped within several yards of the dog, which rolled up its eyes at him.

"Concentrate," Ohlmstead said. "Let the bird straighten out."

Houston took another step; the woodcock rose, zigzagging and twittering, up through the oaks and straightened away. Houston shot and it came down. The dog ran out to get it and brought it back to Ohlmstead, and with a straight face Ohlmstead took it and handed it to Houston.

Houston took it without speaking and stood looking at it as it lay in his hand, and gently stroked the feathers so beautifully arranged for concealment in their blacks and russets and shadowy grays, then looked at Ohlmstead and smiled. "Well," he said, and suddenly his expression changed. "Did you shoot?"

Ohlmstead shook his head.

"Well," Houston said again, and his smile came back. "At last. You know, the one true thing you could have brought up in that cockeyed argument of yours is spiritual satisfaction. I don't know why shooting a bird gives it to me, but I've got it. I think you're responsible, and I'm grateful. Now I think I'll quit for the day. I'll just go along with you."

"I'll quit for the day too," Ohlmstead said. "I've got my grouse."

Houston put the woodcock in his pocket. They shouldered their guns and started for the car with the pointer trotting along in front of them. They were both content as they walked through the fallen leaves with the colors of autumn around them and the fine, faintly bitter smell of autumn in the air.

"Now," Houston said, "maybe the dog will retrieve to me. After two years."

Ohlmstead nodded. He was thinking that Houston had turned out to be a pleasant companion and they would have other good days together. He could feel the weight of the grouse in his game pocket and saw once again, in his mind's eye, the bird's swift and lovely flight up into the opening and his fine shot that had stopped it: an ancient rite of autumn, celebrated in a splendid place.

TWO

THE BUCK was seven years old, coming near his prime, and had lived in the northwest corner of the tract for the last four. He had only been shot at once, in his third year, when he had grown his first small set of antlers that had taken him out of the spike-buck class. This had happened near Twelfth Pool, where he had lived until that time and had often seen men, but after the bullet had smashed into the tree a foot before his face, he had left the vicinity of the stream and moved about until he found the corner, where the cover suited him. There was a lot of thick oak brush eight or ten feet high, very difficult and noisy for men to move about in, scattered hemlocks and pines, several big laurel thickets even more difficult to penetrate than the close-growing oaks, small sunny openings where blueberries grew, and a little spring. It was a perfect place for him, so difficult to enter that grouse hunters only worked the edges and deer hunters avoided it. If anyone tried to ram a way through, the buck could skulk silently around them or lie very close. He had grown more crafty every year of his life and was a master of evasion. A brushy tangle scarcely larger than himself could hide him, he could move through the carpet of fallen leaves without disturbing one of them, and his ears and nose were superb in their power of gathering information, and his eyes were not far behind them. No creature was more adept at keeping out of man's way, as evidenced by his—and other deers—survival in a country where many other creatures had long since been extirpated.

Whitetail deer like small territories and he was as safe within this tangle as he would ever be, so long as he stayed in it, but the mating season was beginning and he was growing restless. The glandular changes of the rut that would send him out to seek the does were swelling his neck and building up a combative spirit in him. The fine set of antlers that had begun to grow in February were now polished and hard and ready for battle with any other buck he might encounter, and he had found a little depression that held some rain water and pawed it out and urinated in it to make a muddy, smelly wallow in which he rolled occasionally.

Two bucks will sometimes keep each other company during the spring and summer, but he had been alone since the herd had left the winter yard and dispersed. When he had encountered other deer, in the forest or in the cultivated fields to the west where most of them went at times by night, he had paid little attention to them. Most of the time it suited him to be alone, but now it did not. First he moved around the edges of the tangle, giving up his habit of only feeding at early morning and toward twilight, and then left it despite the occasional, distant shots of grouse and woodcock hunters.

He headed east toward the stream, alert and staying close to cover, and when he was in the vicinity of the bear's den encountered two grouse close together on the ground. In any other month he would have paid them little attention, but now he paused and snorted at them. One was a cock and chose to object to such a demonstration; it spread its tail, raised its ruffs, puffed out its feathers, and danced toward him. This was enough for the buck, and he lowered his head and charged. The grouse hopped out of the way but continued to dance around him like a bantam rooster and he chased it until on one of his bounds he came close to the hen and frightened it. She flew off, and the cock followed her.

The buck looked after it, stamped a forefoot, and continued on his way. A flock of cedar waxwings went over him in bounding flight, calling in their thin monotone. He came to the spring run above Thirteenth Pool and followed it down to the stream, looked up and down before coming into the open, and drank. He raised his head and stood for a long moment looking up and down the stream, testing the air and with his ears cocked, statuesque with his forward-sweeping antlers against the autumn color of the woods. But nothing moved within his view and the light, shifting breeze was empty of the scent he sought, so he crossed the stream and went on.

A quarter of a mile farther on he came to strong scent. Two does and their fawns had joined each other, as they were likely to do in the fall, and moved off together toward the northern boundary of the tract. They would not be ready for him quite yet and would flee when he caught up with them, but he swung on to their trail and

followed the scent left by the glands on their feet, between the hoofs.

Close to the northern boundary he was brought up short by a man's trail crossing the trail of the does, for Ohlmstead had been out early that morning looking for grouse and had passed that way after the does had gone by and turned back at the stream. The buck threw up his head as though stung, moved back quickly between two large rocks, and stood for a short time listening and searching the vicinity with his eyes. Had he seen a man he would have gone off with long, fluid bounds, making a great, false show of leaving the country; but the man was nowhere in sight and he stole silently away, fading into the nearest cover that would conceal him.

He wouldn't know, and neither would Ohlmstead, that Ohlmstead's morning walk had saved his life that day, for the archery season for deer was open and there was a man with a bow and broadhead arrows in a tree five hundred yards beyond the boundary. The man had come down from the state park farther up the stream; the does had heard him, their ears being five times as acute as his, and turned off. By luck, unaware that he had missed seeing them, he had climbed the tree near their turning point; he was an expert with the bow, and the buck, following the does' trail with his nose to the ground, would have presented him with a fine target.

The moon was nearly full above a high, thin gauze of clouds which diffused its light in a great nacreous disk foretelling the coming storm, and moving about in the ghostly light the night creatures of the tract heard the migrating geese go over. Mellow and resonant, their voices came out of the sky softened by distance, each cry rising a little at the end as though in question, for the geese knew the storm was coming and wanted a sheltered place to wait it out. Perhaps they would pause short of their goal on the slow, meandering river amid the cornfields of Maryland, for they sensed as surely as man knew from his widely gathered data and instruments that the storm would be a bad one.

It had been building up out on the ocean and had reached hurricane force before swinging in toward the southern Atlantic coast; its course had been so erratic that the plotting of it had been changed several times and would be changed several times more. Hurricane warnings were posted, and then it was thought the storm would turn out to sea again; two days after the geese had passed, it swung into Hatteras, moved inland for a few miles, and roared overland to the northeast, cutting a swath of destruction as it went.

The region in which the tract lay escaped the full force of it, but the winds about its periphery filled the forest, the highways, and the streets of the village with fallen branches and many fallen trees; power lines were brought down and lights went out, and for several days those with electric stoves cooked in their fireplaces and went without central heat. The winds were accompanied by torrents of rain beyond anyone's recollection. The river rose toward flood stage, and the stream, above the high-water mark of spring, roared through its bed; from the new road along the tract's eastern boundary, partially graded but not hard-surfaced yet, run-off water cut through the banks and gullied the little valleys running down to the stream, bringing loads of mud.

The dam which made the lake above the tract was also unfinished, because of a strike brought about by a jurisdictional squabble between two union officials fighting for power; the water rose above it, cut channels across its top which quickly deepened, and finally a part of it collapsed and brought down the rest. A wall of raging water came down the stream, undercutting banks and the roots of stream-side trees, rolling great rocks about, scouring the stream bed and shifting it in places, and tearing the bridge from the steel rails that carried it. Nothing was left but the rails. No one had expected such a sudden and violent quirk of nature and hadn't prepared for it, or even considered preparing for it. A strike brought about arbitrarily and needlessly damaged the stream, doing the most harm to the small invertebrate life upon which all other stream life depended. Algae, diatoms, and the larval forms of insects were ground up or washed away, and the larder was greatly diminished.

The larger fish which weren't too far from their ultimate refuges in the cracks running back under the ledges fled into them as the changing pressures and currents gave them short warning of disaster. The others were washed downstream to find themselves in new territories where they didn't know the hiding places, and many were carried up on shore and left to die when the water went down. Even the ones which had avoided the wall of water found their familiar territories changed. The lateral lines down their sides, sensitive to minute and shifting pressures, enabled them to feel their surroundings at a distance, and this had given them a plot of the water around them and cognizance of the other creatures that moved around in it; now all this was changed and unfamiliar and would have to be learned anew. They were hungry and confused and called on their stored fat for nourishment, and the fat gave up its DDT and killed many of them. This would have happened to some of them during the winter in any event, but not to this many. If the dam hadn't gone out, the stress upon them would have been much less.

The old trout in Upper Falls Pool had been secure in his dark labyrinth when the flood came down. The passing of the crest and the suction that followed it tossed him around in his sanctuary, battered him against its stony walls, and drew him out; he could do little to control his movements, for he was very sick. He had eaten a great deal of insecticide and the fungus had spread and crept inexorably inward; his vitality had been lowered to the point where parasitic protozoans had infected him and he was losing his sense of equilibrium. Drawn out into the pool after being beaten against the rock, he reeled languidly about and was washed downstream. His long reign was over, the approaching mating season would take place without him, and another trout would move into his kingdom.

News of the flood water from the broken dam was on the radio early in the morning after the storm, and as soon as he heard it, Ohlmstead started for the tract to see what the damage had been. He was apprehensive of what he was going to find, for he could see that the water had done a good deal of harm even in the low-lying part of the village, which was located on the flats along the river below the gorge that brought the stream down from the hills. He was well aware that higher up, on the tract, the water had been closely confined.

When he came to the highway bridge under which the stream ran after it left the tract, he had the first intimation of how high the water had been, for it had been over the bridge; it had left logs and other trash that the highway crew had already cleared away and piled beside the highway. His heart sank, and he drove to the gate, unlocked it, and drove through. At first the road ran high above the stream and out of sight of it along the side of the ridge, and he drove on for several hundred yards until he came to a tree that had fallen across the road. He had to leave the car there. There was another tree a little farther on, and then he began to descend the hill until the road leveled off where the little floodplain began near Bridge Pool. The water had swept over it, gullying the road, leaving logs, branches, and bunches of dead leaves hung in the brush and the floodplain itself scoured down to its rocky floor. He went on until he came to the bridge. It was gone, nothing left of it but the two steel rails which had carried the bridge itself, and the concrete abutments on each side that held the rails. Below it, Bridge Pool had been so changed that he hardly recognized it. Great rocks had been shifted, a course or two had been washed off the top of the rock dam and the stream had dropped, one bank had been undercut, and several fine hemlocks were leaning drunkenly over the stream. Presently they would fall into it if they weren't taken down. Looking at all this, Ohlmstead had a feeling almost of unbelief, for he had known and fished the old pool for so long that it had come to seem as immutable as the rocky ridges that surrounded it; it was as though he had lost something he had never thought to lose.

He slowly turned away from it and looked upstream, to find that changed as much; the strange feeling of unbelief grew even stronger, for the reach above the bridge had always been one of his favorites. It was longer than the reach below, three pools could be seen from it, and every time he came into the tract he stopped on the bridge to look at it, to watch the clear water spilling white over the dams between the timbered banks; the view had always typified for him the largely untouched beauty of the tract, where he truly felt a part of the earth he stood upon that in so many other places had been plundered and abused.

As he stood there the feeling of unbelief gradually gave way to rational thought, for he was a rational man; he had had his moment of shock and was ready to get on with what had to be done. The first question that came to his mind was why this had happened, but it was characteristic that he pushed it into the back of his mind to be taken care of in due course. He turned away from the two lonely rails spanning the water and picked his way downstream for a quarter of a mile through the detritus of the flood and, greatly depressed by what he saw, climbed the hill to his car and drove to the village.

He went first to see Joe Borrow, the man who had built their road and did work for them on the tract. Borrow, a short, barrel-chested man in coveralls, was just coming out the door as Ohlmstead pulled up in front of the house, and came over to the car. He was still chewing a piece of toast.

"Hi," he said. "Had a flood, eh? You seen them two houses down on the flat?"

"No," Ohlmstead said. "At least, only from a distance. I've been up on the stream."

"I'll bet it's a mess. All that water cooped up, something had to give."

"It did," Ohlmstead said grimly. "There will be a lot of work to do. There are two trees down across the road before the bridge, the road's pretty well washed out in spots, and the bridge is gone."

"No!" Borrow said. "The rails, too? I didn't think them rails would ever go, sunk like they are in concrete."

"They're all that's left. Can you get up there and clear the road and fix it, and get the bridge in again? Then we can see what things look like beyond it."

"Sure," Borrow said. "I'll start today. What's the stream look like?"

"I don't even want to talk about it," Ohlmstead said. "It's so changed. Dams, banks, everything. You'll see."

"It's a goddam shame," Borrow said. "A pretty stream like that. It ain't that the guys had any beef, either. They didn't want to strike."

"What?" Ohlmstead said, sitting up. "Who didn't want to strike? What's a strike got to do with it?"

"They struck on the dam, before it was finished, and that's why it washed out. Didn't you know that?"

"No," Ohlmstead said. "It wasn't on the radio. They've already started to cover up, if that's the case. How did you know?"

"I got a second cousin workin' up there, he told me. He was at my house yesterday on account of he wasn't workin'. He said a union steward told them not to let it get around, but he told me. They're back now, they got pulled back quick after what happened. Like I say, they didn't want to strike. It was a fight between the union brass about who was to run the show, and they called the strike."

Ohlmstead stared at him, so outraged by this callous irresponsibility that at first he couldn't find words to express what he felt. His fists clenched, and if these men had been there, he would have assaulted them. A knock on the head was apparently the only thing that would stop such people and others like them in their single-minded scramble for money or power. "The bastards," he said. "Oh, the bastards."

"Yeah," Borrow said. "You're right."

Ohlmstead looked down and saw his clenched fists, shook his head, and relaxed. The damage was done, and he wouldn't get anywhere that way; there were enough fools doing it already for reasons that were stupid or misguided or perhaps even tenable, and he wanted no part of that. A thought, half-formed, that he should have done something before, beyond the narrow confines of the tract, occurred to him, but he pushed it back; he had enough to do at the moment and would get at it later. He looked up. "Joe," he said, "I'll have to get along. After you get the bridge fixed we'll walk the stream and see what has to be done, and it'll be plenty. I'll see you up there."

"Okay," Borrow said.

Ohlmstead drove home and put in a call for Goodenow in Philadelphia. "Hello, Alec," he said, when Goodenow got on the line. "I've got nothing but bad news, so brace yourself. Have you heard anything about what's been going on up here?"

"There was something on the radio about flood damage in the village, so I wondered. I thought I'd hear from you. Let's have it."

Ohlmstead gave it to him: the condition of the stream so far as he had seen it, and the reason for what had happened as Borrow had reported it to him.

There was a silence, and then Goodenow said: "My God." There was another silence, and he added: "Besides the rest of it, the bottom's been pretty well scoured, from what you say."

"Yes," Ohlmstead said. "I don't know what the effect's been on the bottom life, but it couldn't have been good. I don't know how much food's left for the trout; there must have been a hell of a lot of insect life and other stuff carried away. The thing came about spawning time, and a lot of fish have been moved out of their territories or carried ashore and left there or washed off the tract maybe. We won't know how bad it will be until next spring, when the fishing starts again. And then there was the spray to further confuse the situation. It will take a couple of years to tell what the effect of it all was on the hatch of young trout. Some of the banks—I don't know how many yet—that have been stabilized for years have gone. Probably all the rock dams will need pushing up again, and we won't be able to get a bulldozer in for that until low water next summer. There will be a hell of a lot of work, Alec, and it'll be damned expensive. We ought to be compensated by the state."

"I'll knock myself out seeing that we are," Goodenow said, "and I'll get the stream improvement committee up there as soon as I can to walk the stream with you and begin to plan for what we'll have to do. In the meantime, would you mind if I appointed you a committee of one to get things going that have to be done right away?"

"I've got Borrow started on the bridge, and after that's finished we'll open the road from there and get the trees down that have been undercut. I'll be working along with him, I guess. If anybody wants to come up this weekend, we can rent a couple of power saws."

"I'll call around and get you some volunteers," Goodenow said. "We'll stop at your house, and we can all go to the stream together. I'll see if I can have a state man there too."

"Okay," Ohlmstead said, and asked, "Have you heard any more about the pipeline?"

"Rothiker hasn't come up with anything yet, and I haven't either. If they've made up their minds to come through us, I don't think we can stop them, but we'll try. We'll just have to hope for a bit of luck, but the way things have been going . . ." He was silent for a moment. "And all of it unnecessary."

"As unnecessary as turning Lake Erie into a stinking cesspool," Ohlmstead said. "Well, Alec, I'll be in touch with you. Goodbye."

"Goodbye, Jerry, and thanks."

Ohlmstead was on the stream again that afternoon and walked most of it; he was shocked and depressed by what he saw, and wrote Goodenow fully about it that night. He couldn't get there the next day, having some business of his own that had to be attended to, but the day after that he drove to the stream to see how Borrow was progressing with the bridge and lend a hand. Borrow was working on the planking, which was three-quarters of the way across, and walked over when Ohlmstead pulled up. "Sure a mess, ain't it?" he said. "It don't look like the same creek." He shook his head. "Well, I ought to be finished with the flooring today or tomorrow. Then I can get the road from here usable before I put the guard rails up. That okay?"

"Sure," Ohlmstead said. "I'll work along with you, Joe. Some of the boys will be up this weekend to lend a hand, and at least we'll get the road cleaned up. Nobody can drive up there until the road's back in shape anyhow. I doubt there'll be much traffic in here until the deer season. I've sort of passed the word around that we shouldn't kill any more grouse this year."

"Yeah," Borrow said. "The way I hear it, the grouse ain't been too good anywhere they sprayed with that airplane." He spat.

"Oh," he said. "You got fish trouble, too. I been seein' dead ones floatin' by."

"What?" Ohlmstead said, startled. "Dead trout? My God, what next? How long's this been going on?"

"Well, yesterday evenin' and this mornin'. I meant to call you and tell you, but then somebody came in and we had a few beers."

"It's just recent, then, it's not from the storm. What the hell could be doing it? Do you know of anything going on up the stream?"

"They're workin' on the dam again, is all I know. Guy who was in last night told me they were blastin' up there to get more rock."

"Blasting up there wouldn't kill fish down here," Ohlmstead said. In his concern he began to tap on the back of one hand with the fingers of the other. "They couldn't be using some kind of chemical . . . No. Can you think of anything, Joe? I've got to get up there, but what do you think could be the cause of it?"

Borrow stared at him for a moment, then took off his battered hat and scratched his head. "Well," he said finally. "Up around Mauch Chunk, where I came from, we used to get mine drainage that would kill fish. It's like acid, it'll sure kill hell out of the fish." Still staring at Ohlmstead, his eyes a little unfocused in the effort of remembering, he put his hat on again. "By damn, you know there's a little mine up on the hillside up near that dam, I saw it a couple of times when I was deer huntin' up that way before I got the sciatica, and maybe the blastin' has shook a crack in the rocks and let the old mine water out. The old mine never was sealed off, like it should have been. It was just a little old mine anyhow. Two, three guys worked it for a while, back there—"

"That's it," Ohlmstead said, interrupting him. "Joe, that's it. Oh, those left-footed bastards, they probably never looked around enough to find it. I've got to get up there right away, I'll see you later. Where was the mine?"

"On the west side of the creek, a little down this way from the dam. Kinda high up. Okay, I hope you get it stopped. I'll see you."

Ohlmstead turned and trotted to his car and drove out of the tract. He stopped at his house long enough to call Goodenow and tell him what was happening, what he was going to do, and suggest that Goodenow call the state capital at once, and took off for the dam.

When he was halfway there, preoccupied with worry about the effect of the drainage on top of everything else, a siren began to wail behind him and a state trooper in a patrol car pulled up beside him and gestured for him to stop. He cursed and pulled off the highway; the trooper stopped behind him and walked up to his car. Ohlmstead knew the man, whose name was Tom something or other; he had occasionally had a beer with him after hours in the village, and hoped that would help.

"Hi, Mr. Ohlmstead," the trooper said. "I hate to pull you over, but you were doing sixty-eight and the limit's fifty-five. Speed kills, Mr. Ohlmstead. You got your license?"

Ohlmstead searched around for his license, butterfingered with frustration and longing to say that speed wasn't the only thing that killed when any numskull who could drive around a pole at five miles an hour and pay a small fee was forthwith turned loose to gambol with three hundred horsepower, but he forbore and produced his license. The trooper looked at it carefully. "Like I said, Mr. Ohlmstead, speed kills," he said, "and you're a good driver, you've never been tagged. You got an emergency, maybe?"

"I think so, Tom. I just found out that they're blasting at the new dam and they've opened up an old mine that's draining into our stream, killing fish and raising hell. The mine acid will go on down into the river and raise hell there too. We've called the state, but I'm not sure the state can get them on the phone up there, so I thought I'd better jump up and give them the word."

Tom considered this carefully, while Ohlmstead's fingers played a silent tattoo on his knee. "Yeah," Tom said finally. "It sure don't sound good. You say you called the state?"

"Just before I left."

To Ohlmstead's vast relief, Tom came to a decision. "Okay, then," he said. "We better get going. You stay behind me and I'll get you up there."

He returned to his car, swung around Ohlmstead's, and, with an occasional blast of the siren, they roared up the road, Ohlmstead telling himself in sardonic amusement that speed kills and they were both dead men. When they reached the construction road into the dam the trooper swung about, raised a hand, and went on his way.

There was a state car near the construction shack and as Ohlmstead pulled up beside it a man came out of the shack and walked over to him.

"Ohlmstead," Ohlmstead said, getting out of his car. "From the club down the stream. We're getting mine drainage. You the foreman?"

"Gregory, Mr. Ohlmstead," the man said, putting out his hand. "I'm from the state. They got a phone call from Philly and caught me on the radio about five miles down the road and I ducked up here. I've sent the whole crew out to check around, and I'll join them in a minute. I've been on the phone to the office."

Ohlmstead had been prepared for argument, buck-passing, and delay and was ready to take a strong line. The swiftness with which action had been started took some of the wind out of his sails, but the man was being far from candid and Ohlmstead said: "It's good to know they can move fast when they want to, but why didn't they seal the mine off sooner?"

"Oh," Gregory said. His eyes opened wider; it was evident that he was rather startled that Ohlmstead knew about the mine, but he quickly recovered from his surprise. "The mine. We think it could have been the mine, and we're going to seal that right away, before the next rain."

"Didn't they know it was there?"

"They must have, I'm sure they did," Gregory said. He looked around and dropped his voice a little. "It must be on our maps, but you know how it is. People are careless, they don't pay as much attention to their jobs as they used to. Frankly, I think it was over-looked somehow. Some engineer forgot about it and it got left out, and then when they started blasting . . . Only please don't quote me personally. I need the job."

"I won't quote you," Ohlmstead said. "There's no need for it anyhow. D'you know Joe Borrow, in the village?" Gregory nodded. "Joe knew about the mine, and when he saw the dead fish floating by, he called it." Gregory didn't reply, and Ohlmstead went on: "Maybe it wasn't an engineer, maybe they took a chance that the mine would hold water forever and that blasting wouldn't open the rock, and tried to save a little money. It's been done before, it's being done all the time. I doubt we'll ever know, but between the spraying and this mess we've lost a lot of fish—probably most of

180

them—and it'll probably take years for the ecology of the stream to come back."

"I'm sure the Fish Commission will do what has to be done to repair the damage," Gregory said.

"We'll do our best to see that they do—and everything will be complicated by the damage done when the dam went out."

"But that was an act of God," Gregory said. "I don't see how anyone could hold us for that. The hurricane—"

"No," Ohlmstead said. "Not the hurricane, the union brass. If your people take the act-of-God line we will bring up the irresponsible strike at a time when the autumn storms were due, and the fact that no other dam gave way. If it did, it hasn't been reported. Your people hired the work done, and are responsible; union or not, you should have made some provisions to protect everyone downstream."

Gregory shook his head but didn't say anything; he saw that Ohlmstead had the facts. He looked at the ground for a moment. "All that will be out of my hands," he said finally, looking up again. "My job is to get that damned mine sealed off as soon as possible, and then I'm through."

Ohlmstead, sure that he had got across that they knew what they were talking about and that this would be reported, let it go. "We do appreciate how quickly you got on to this," he said. "Many thanks." They shook hands, and as Ohlmstead turned away another thought struck him. "Have you heard anything about a pipeline coming through here?" he asked, turning again.

Gregory was walking toward the shack; he paused and when he turned his face was blank. He shook his head and walked on.

Ohlmstead walked to his car, got in, and headed for home. For a few miles he felt pleased about Goodenow's getting such prompt action and about his own talk with Gregory, for he had scotched any dissembling about the cause of the trouble and that would save time, frustration, and expense in their negotiations with bureaucracy, and he had clearly indicated that they would fight if they had to. Presently, however, a great sense of depression settled down on him and stayed with him the rest of the way.

The sun was going down when he reached home, and he put the car away and walked slowly through the long, chill shadows and fallen leaves on the lawn to the house. The kitchen was warm and a little steamy and pleasant with cooking smells and Mrs. McIntyre was bustling around; she'd laid and lit a fire in the living room, and after speaking to her he went in and warmed his back at it before returning to the kitchen to make himself a drink.

"Those nasty squirrels," she said. "They've been trying to get into the bird feeder again, and I went out and chased them with the broom."

Ohlmstead took the first sip of the drink and felt the whiskey warm in his belly; his depression lifted a little. "That's the spirit," he said absently, and drank again.

Mrs. McIntyre paused in her attentions to the stove and looked at him. "I declare," she said, "but you do look down in the mouth."

Ohlmstead sat down at the kitchen table. "I've had a depressing day," he said, and decided he didn't want to talk about it. To go into a long exposition, which she doubtless wouldn't understand anyhow, would only bring back the depression that the whiskey had in a small measure dispelled. "Don't ask me about it," he said, "and it might go away."

"Ha!" she said. "You sound like my mother. When we were little and there was a thing we ought to do and didn't want to, she used to say if we didn't look at it it mightn't be there any more. It was, though." He nodded, and she decided to cheer him up. "George Simpson broke his leg on Tuesday."

He looked at her and saw by her expression that she was about to embark on another of her village tales. It would be a distraction, and he decided to play along. "Why, poor George," he said. "I guess the Lord finally looked the other way."

"It was high time, too," she said, and nodded with satisfaction. George's numerous escapes from lethal damage during his occasional heroic bouts with the bottle had aroused a certain local envy, for no one else had enjoyed such durable good fortune; in her opinion Providence had been entirely too long-suffering with him. "High time," she said again.

"I can't but agree, but the leg . . . ?"

"Well, he called my John and wanted to go goose shooting."

"Goose shooting around here? Where?"

"He'd seen some geese on that little pond over near Bethel, or said he had. I tried to talk my John out of it, but he wouldn't listen to me, so he went. Well, my John said George wasn't feeling any pain and he thought he'd stay out of range of him, so he dropped him on one side of the pond and went around to the other. When he got through the bushes there was one goose out in the middle of it, and it got up and flew over George about a mile in the air and George shot it."

"And it fell on him?"

"Oh, not it. When my John got back to him he was out on the road carrying it by the neck. My John said he asked him how he managed to hit it, it was so high, and he said how could he miss it in a flock as big as that? Can you imagine? He certainly was in good shape. It's a wonder somebody didn't get shot."

"Both George's legs were still in good shape?" Ohlmstead asked.

"Now don't rush me," Mrs. McIntyre said. "It wasn't then. They were driving back, and George took a bottle out of his back pocket and had a couple more because he had a goose, and then they came to that concrete bridge over Bethel Creek and there was a concrete mixer standing there with a man beside it. The man waved for them to stop, and George made my John stop and got out and talked to him."

"Mrs. Mac—" Ohlmstead had started to wonder whether he'd missed something somewhere.

"Now you just wait a minute. The man said he was waiting for his truck to haul the mixer away but that he didn't have much use for it for a while and had a mind to sell it if George was interested. George said sure, he could use it if the price was right. My John began to smell a rat about then and tried to talk George out of it, but George shushed him and wouldn't listen and paid the man forty-five dollars and the man took the money and walked away. Then George climbed up on the mixer and staggered around and told my John what a good deal he'd got, and just then the state truck came up."

"It was the state's mixer?" Ohlmstead asked.

"Did you ever? They'd left it there when they were fixing the bridge. When they got George convinced it was their mixer, he started to yell and stamp around on top of it and tripped and fell off. That's when he broke his leg."

Ohlmstead burst out laughing and she laughed with him. When

184

their merriment over George's misfortune had subsided somewhat she said: "The man that took his money had escaped from the county jail, and they haven't found him yet." They laughed again. "There now," Mrs. McIntyre said presently, "you feel better, even if George had to break his leg to do it. Your dinner's ready, you better go sit down."

Ohlmstead went into the dining room and enjoyed his dinner, cheered through the meal by the story and the imagined scene. When he had finished he moved into the living room again and read the paper by the fire. Mrs. McIntyre finished clearing up and put her head around the door.

"I'll go now. I'll see you tomorrow."

"Good night," Ohlmstead said. "If you see George, tell him it looks to me as though his luck has finally run out."

They grinned at each other and she withdrew her head, which reappeared again almost at once. "I forgot to tell you," she said. "When my John got home from taking George to the hospital they called him from the Seneca. They're going to start a ski slide like everybody else is doing and stay open all winter next year."

"Did they call him to tell him that?"

"Oh, no. They want him to bid."

"Bid?" Ohlmstead asked. "Bid on what?"

"They'll need a new sewer thing, the one they have won't be big enough. They don't have any more room on their side, they're going to put it on that piece of land they own on your side. I meant to tell you."

"Ah!" Ohlmstead said. He felt as though someone had stabbed him between the ribs. "Thank you. Thanks, Mrs. Mac."

"Good night," she said, and disappeared.

Left alone, he put the paper down and stared unseeing into the fire as he assimilated the day's final blow. The Seneca's piece of land on their side of the road was well above them, but from there the land sloped down; the "sewer thing," the settling basin and treatment plant, would send its effluent down into the stream. The effluent would be clear, there were laws about that. But as Ohlmstead saw it (and he had looked into it because of the prospective development along the new road to the dam), while there were other laws to regulate the effluent's phosphorus, nitrogen, and other organic content that would change the water's character and greatly encourage the growth of algae and other undesirable life, these laws were rarely enforced. And what if the thing broke down, or they scamped occasionally on the operation to save a few dollars . . .

In his mind's eye he saw the fine clear pools and the clean rocky banks (or what was left of them at the moment) choked with ugly thick filamentous green mats or greenish scum. Perhaps in his deep despondency he made the picture too somber; perhaps the water would remain too cold, despite being warmed as it lay behind the dam, to support such growth; but he knew what had happened to too many other rivers and streams to be optimistic, and had watched the operations of too many developers and quick profit-takers who plundered the land, and politicians after money or votes. For the tract the process of degradation had begun, and he had little hope that it would cease; for although conservationists were gaining in strength and effectiveness, their battle had really only started. Industry was culpable, but the ultimate basis was the individual, and the individual in the main had not joined the battle yet.

It wasn't only the Seneca; it was everything. Their little enclave,

Ohlmstead thought with grief and melancholy, was a fading symbol of the past, put together by men who took delight in nature and derived a satisfaction of spirit from her; it was an anachronism, changing now into a symbol of a different time.

The woodcock that had come in the spring to the little swamp between Fifth and Sixth Pools was still on the tract; Ohlmstead's plan to hunt him up had been frustrated by the weather, and nobody else had stumbled across him. A few hours before the storm he had grown sufficiently uneasy to move his daytime roosting place to a tangle of old windfall timber, grown thick with briars, farther down the hill. It was here that he sat out the storm, protected from the wild rain and wilder wind that dropped branches on the old fallen tree above his head.

After it was clear again he left this place, which was too damp to suit him; his old roosting place was too damp as well, and he finally found a new place to his liking on top of the ridge near the sphagnum bog. The weather grew colder and calm after the storm had gone its way, and there was frost in the mornings. It was close to the time for him to leave, but the ridge top got more sun than the valley and cold-air drainage down the slope left the ground softer than it was below and he stayed on.

Almost all the leaves were down now but the sun was warm during the days in his sheltered spot; perhaps there was a reluctance in him to leave the familiar ground and embark on the long and often hazardous flight to the south that he had taken so often, and the impulse to go was not so urgent as the stirring summons of spring. He never saw either of his little family of the summer, for his mate had been shot in the second week of the season by one of the members and the young bird had moved farther down the stream.

Other creatures with which he had grown familiar were vanishing. The several bats that he had often seen wheeling in erratic flight in the gloaming had given up their hunting as insects grew scarce, and now hung head-down with others which had come in from a distance in the dark recesses of their cave in hibernation, wrapped in their wings, with heartbeat, respiration, and metabolism slowed down. Snakes had retreated to entwine and sleep the winter away, and groundhogs fat from summer feeding were curled up underground. Frogs had burrowed down into the mud, but raccoons were still about; they would wait a while longer before giving up the world for a time.

Between his feeding flights he napped away the sunny hours, often waking to awareness of the life around him. Field mice, deer mice, rabbits, a few birds, and an occasional shrew went their ways. A marsh hawk sometimes appeared and quartered the bog; one day a four-year-old buck from several miles to the west wandered into the far edge of the bog and the old buck, who had come sniffing that way, found him. Full of ire, they had charged each other like rams, with their heads down, and their antlers met with a crash. For a long moment they were locked together and the young buck was brought down on his hocks. Exhaustion and starvation faced them, but the old buck broke the lock with a savage twist, the young one got his hind feet under him, and they dug in their hoofs and strove against each other with all their strength, tearing up the ground and grunting and gasping for breath. As they strained and fenced for an opening to stab one another the clashing of their antlers brought many creatures out to watch the battle.

The young buck fought well, but the old one's superior weight and experience in combat were too much for him; he finally turned away and fled, and the old one pursued him far enough to be out of the woodcock's hearing. Quiet descended again and a little later a doe, attracted by the sounds of the fray, stole past his cover. Later still, a bank of clouds covered the sun and a chilly little wind came up and plucked at the dry leaves not yet fallen. The old bear and the cubs, which had been a mile away and had heard the far-carrying clash of battle, moved toward it and came up behind the woodcock; one cub caught his scent and followed it merely for the pleasure of stirring the bird up.

The woodcock sat attentive and still until the cub was about six feet away and ready to pounce and then jumped into the air, zigzagged up through the brush, and straightened away for another nearby cover; halfway there, however, he changed his mind, rose higher in the air, and setting his course for the south left the chilly little wind and the dry ticking of leaves behind.

THREE

For a time after the flood crest had gone by, stranding many trout in the little hollows back from the banks of the stream, the raccoons from the old tree above Bear Swamp were busy taking advantage of such an unusual windfall. They were still together as a family and would be until the following spring, for they got along well together, seeming to enjoy each other's company; occasionally one of them would wander off and sleep alone, but usually they were together during the day, curled up close and keeping each other warm. If the days were sunny and the wind not too cold they could still be found sprawled over the high limbs of a single tree taking their sun baths in the warmest part of the day.

The stranded trout were a fortunate accident, filling a time when frogs were hard to find, helping them to lay on fat for the winter and the lean hungry days of early spring when they came out of their semi-hibernation. Presently, however, the trout were gone and they turned to hunting for the crawfish hiding under submerged stones along the banks, but the flood's scouring of the bottom had killed many of the fish and the mine drainage, on top of it, had killed many more. Besides, the raccoons had been along the stream when the mine drainage came down and its smell and taste caused them to shy away from it. First many of the tasty insects of summer had vanished after the spraying, and now the stream as they had always known it, a fine hunting ground and unfailing source of good things, was changed. Although they had a tendency, like most raccoons, to wander more widely in the fall, the stream had even then been the center of their peregrinations; now they drifted away from it.

Their erratic course took them roughly toward the northwest, across the stream; when they reached the end of the swamp from which came the spring run that entered the stream between Fifth and Sixth Pools they met the old male porcupine from west of the tract. The mating urge was on him and he was wandering out of his usual territory too, whining and moaning to himself in his discontent because he hadn't as yet found a mate. Two of the young raccoons were off in the woods somewhere, but the other young one and the old pair were together and somehow seemed to agree that it would be entertaining to bait the old porcupine. The old male approached it from the front, puffing himself up and moving sideways toward it; the other two moved off a little to each side.

The porcupine stopped, puzzled; raccoons had never given it any trouble before, and its slow brain didn't comprehend what was happening. Its temper was short and it wanted to get on with its search; it had been minding its own affairs and suddenly seemed to be surrounded by hostile raccoons. The male, with his fur and ringed tail fluffed out, was almost as big as it was and was making short sidewise rushes as though to attack and then withdrawing only to advance again. It could have got him out of the·way by swinging about and backing toward him with a flailing tail, but then it would have exposed its head to the other two, which made demonstrations of their own when it edged toward them. With its quills erected, gnashing its teeth and growling, it looked about for a stone or root under which it could get its head and could see neither and screeched with rage, anxiety, and frustration.

The raccoons, thoroughly enjoying themselves, divided its attention with their maneuvers; but it finally saw that there was a tree near the young one, swung about, and backed in that direction with its tail flailing. The young raccoon hopped out of the way; the porcupine reached the tree and using its tail alternately as a prop and a threat climbed the trunk. The raccoons drew together and watched it, and the old dog fox from off the tract, which had been prowling over the next hill and had heard the porcupine scream, came galloping up to see what the uproar was about, sat down, and watched them all. The porcupine reached a crotch and settled peevishly into it; the raccoons looked at the fox, the fox looked at the raccoons, and after a moment, seeing that the game was over, all went their ways.

Later in the night the three raccoons were joined by the other two, and a little before dawn they reached the bog on the ridge and after some exploration found a good hollow in an old black walnut in which to spend the day. Two nights later they reached the farm to the west where the young horned owl had been brought to

disaster, for the old male, who had been there in his lonely summer wanderings before he joined the family again, remembered the good feeding he had found and led them back.

The weather was suddenly turning colder and there was little in the fields for them now; the corn that hadn't been harvested was hard and dry, the few unpicked tomatoes were frosted, and the pumpkins didn't attract them. The two which had wandered off before wandered off again, and the other three came into the wind, which was blowing from the house, and were enticed that way by the mixture of interesting scents that the wind brought them. The two farm dogs were off hunting by themselves and consequently didn't interfere with them, and they fanned out and assiduously began their investigations.

The young one found the garbage can, managed to pry the lid up and get into it, and fell happily to stuffing itself at about the same time that the old pair got into the henhouse. The old male climbed up on the roost and grabbed a young pullet that was the nearest thing to him; its flapping wings and squawks of pain and fright instantly sent the other chickens into such a pandemonium that the young raccoon in the garbage can jumped and dislodged the lid. It fell back into place with a clang, imprisoning him inside the can, and he began a noisy, snarling fight to get out.

The farmer had been pouring himself a cup of coffee in the kitchen; at the sudden uproar he grabbed an iron frying pan from the stove and ran cursing out the back door. As he came out, the garbage can tipped over and the young raccoon scuttled out of it and vanished into the shadows, giving him a start. He raised the frying pan to throw after it, decided to hold on to it, and ran to the henhouse and yanked the door open. A great hullabaloo met him.

In the dusty darkness the chickens were squawking and flying blindly into the walls and each other; one flew into him, almost knocking him down, and the two raccoons scrambled past him, one between his legs and the other over his foot. He stumbled about and swung wildly and ineffectually with the frying pan, and a moment later got the door shut and stood with his back against it, cursing himself that he had been startled into running out without a light and his shotgun.

The raccoons made off in the direction they had come and before morning were all together again. They slept through the day in the old black walnut near the bog, and as the temperature was steadily dropping, inducing in them a common inclination to renounce the world for a time, they started the next evening for their old hollow tree above Bear Swamp Run.

The old male porcupine had crossed the stream and finally found the female that had lost its young one to Houston's pointer close to the swamp near Hemlock Pool; moved by an urge like his own, she had wandered several miles from her own territory. He had caught a drift of her scent on the shifting breeze back from the stream, confusing because he couldn't pinpoint her location, and climbing to the top of a sloping rock sang his querulous, quavering, mournful love song. It sounded like the crying of a human infant in the wintry woods, but she heard it and sought him out. Their meeting was a solemn one and their expressions showed no change from their usual stolid cast, but they touched noses and presently, standing on their hind legs, walked clumsily about each other in a sort of lugubrious dance.

Now that they had found each other, they were inseparable and would be for a week or so, and in no hurry to bring their meeting to a consummation. They moved around together, snuffling and chattering, climbing the same trees, and slept side by side in some secluded place in the daytime—a most unusual state of affairs for the most solitary of animals. Little disturbed them in their unhurried progress, and even the buck, now at the height of his own mating season and quite ready to take on all comers when he met them, limited himself to stamping, snorting, and lowering his rack toward them before going on his way. Invincibly armed with more than thirty thousand quills apiece and well aware of it, occasionally indulging in a bit of solemn play, they wandered about the tract. When the time for love-making came, the female didn't roll over on her back or crawl belly-up out on some branch for the male to walk over her, as the legends had it, but raised herself on her four legs, held her tail to one side, and relaxed her quills. The male approached her with due care, standing on his hind legs. Even in this high moment their expressions didn't change.

In all probability they would mate again within the next few hours before they separated to take up their solitary lives anew and spend most of the winter in the trees, gnawing through to the inner bark of the hemlocks, sugar maples, and beeches that sustained them.

The bear and her cubs were sleek and round with the season's bounty, which they had been eating practically around the clock to lay on fat for the winter's hibernation. During the autumn they had wandered for some distance off the tract, beyond their usual territory, but as the weather grew colder they had gradually worked their way back toward the old den. Once they were back in the old familiar territory they were content to stay pretty much within it, taking life easy and loafing about.

The cubs had grown a good deal and had learned some discretion; their first youthful exuberance had by now been tempered by experience and their mother's discipline. They were still playful, but no longer bounced into dubious situations with the abandon of early youth. Well fed and full of vitality, they had the clownish good nature that is characteristic of happy, undisturbed black bears; they wrestled by the hour, bright-eyed and grinning, tumbling and rolling about, with as great a variety of holds as experienced human wrestlers could invent. When one of them had enough for a time he would break away and run for a tree, climbing it by upward leaps like a cat, corkscrewing around the trunk. They both loved to climb and once aloft would sometimes lie on their backs on big limbs, pushing against the trunks with their hind feet to slide out and perhaps lose their balance and drop to the limb below. They seemed almost as accomplished as monkeys in their antics high above the earth.

That there were still two of them despite the mischances of life was a tribute to the old bear's care, and now that she had managed to instill a measure of prudence in them and brought them along so far, she was able to relax somewhat herself, except when it came to men. She never relaxed her vigilance when it came to these dangerous creatures or missed an opportunity to impress her fear of them on the cubs. She had several chances to do this. The archery season for deer had closed after running for a month and hunters had been in the woods; there would be more during the two-week rifle season for bucks, as that had opened when the other closed. When the wind was right the old bear could scent a man half a mile away.

Even coming across the trail of one in the darkness sent her off with a gruff and urgent summons for the cubs to follow her, and her reaction was always so quick and unmistakable that by now they were sharing it with her. They were becoming as adept as she at remaining invisible to men, as ready to vanish silently as shadows far ahead of them.

These times, however, were the exception rather than the rule, particularly if they stayed within the boundaries of the tract, for the members who hunted deer (none of whom was an archer) stayed away from the ankle-twisting area of the den, while the bears stayed closer to it as the weather grew colder and hibernation time approached.

The old bear had already carried several armfuls of leaves into the den and occasionally took in more. This went on in a leisurely way, for she was in no hurry; insulated by her fur and a fine layer of fat, she was having a lazy time after a long and busy one of bringing up the cubs. She spent many hours close to the den, often on the lip of the ledge behind the tangle of down timber from which she had first seen the snow-patched woods in the spring. She would sprawl on her back at ease, one forepaw in her mouth, mumbling and murmuring in contentment. The cubs gamboled and scuffled around her, sometimes taking hold of her in play and sometimes being lazy themselves; once in a while they made short excursions of their own. One time they stumbled upon the old male porcupine moving from one tree to another as he slowly made his way back to his own territory. They tried cautiously to induce him to play with them, but aside from erecting his quills when they moved in where he considered them too close, he paid them little other attention.

After the flood had passed, they had found some of the stranded fish and eaten them and caught some suckers after the water went down again, but since the mine drainage with its evil smell and taste came down they avoided the stream. One afternoon they were moved to look at it once more. They weren't eating much now, if anything, for they would begin their hibernation within a few days and would go in with their bellies and intestines empty; it would probably be their last trip away from the den and not a very long one at that, but they had chosen an unfortunate time for it. The two-day bear season had opened the day before, and the man who had missed the shot at the old buck because of Ohlmstead's early-morning walk was in the tree near the stream several hundred yards beyond the tract's northern boundary.

He had finally killed a doe from his tree in the archery season, and in his moving around he had found bear excrement in several places. He remembered the talk in the village several years before when the old bear's mother had been killed, and the more recent tale of the two boys being frightened at the dump, and was sure that the bears were still in the vicinity. He had wanted to kill a bear for years, and as the tree from which he had shot the doe was near a deer trail which he thought might be used by the bears he was in the tree again.

The wind was coming from behind the bears as they moved along the stream and crossed it on the fallen tree that the members used as a footbridge during the high water of spring. Once across, they took the deer trail, crossed the tract's boundary, and continued on. The cubs were playing together off the trail, wrestling and tumbling about, when the arrow flickered between the trees and buried itself almost to the feathers between the old bear's ribs. She stumbled and fell, bawling with shock and pain, got up again, and whirling about ran back the way she had come with the suddenly frightened cubs after her. She ran blindly on, upheld for a little time by her splendid vitality, but she was mortally hit; the familiar woods were fading to darkness and she would never see again the cubs she had loved and chastened or the den beneath the ledge.

The weekend after Ohlmstead had phoned Goodenow seven members had come up and helped with the road and the trees, the stream-improvement committee had reviewed the damage, made some plans, talked to Borrow, and gone home to plan some more; Ohlmstead himself spent every day on the stream working with Borrow.

During this time, as he had talked to the other men or worked along with Borrow trying to retrieve a little of what had been lost, he had gone through a variety of emotions. At first there had been a sort of numbed disbelief, almost as it had been when he lost his wife, for after her he loved the stream and the tract more than anything else in the world and the stream as he had known and loved it had been broken up for a long time to come. This had gradually changed to a simmering rage against the disasters and the perpetrators of these disasters that he had been unable to control, that woke him cursing in the night or flared up into an irritability which sent Mrs. McIntyre around on tiptoe with an expression of patient injury.

Presently, however, being a rational man, he saw the futility of continuing down this dark cul-de-sac and made his way out of it, feeling a little ashamed and apologizing to Mrs. McIntyre. He was certainly not happy after he had done this, but at least he had come to a sort of forlorn peace with himself. He put it all out of his mind for a time and took refuge in hard physical exercise, working with Borrow; being out in the air, struggling with recalcitrant rocks and trees and machinery and using his muscles, was the best thing he could have done.

An overcast had blotted out the stars by midnight, and an hour later it began to snow. The flakes, small and tentative at first, soon increased in size and number until they seemed to fill the air between the bare maples and gather on the sweeping branches of the hemlocks, silently turning the forest white.

It was still snowing when Ohlmstead got out of bed the next morning to lower his window. He had slept quite late, an unusual thing for him, and as he stood looking out at the falling snow he thought that this winter he might go south for a time. The newscast the night before had indicated that the storm would last all day and probably longer; if it did they wouldn't be able to get into the tract. Their work had come to a stop, possibly until spring, unless the weather changed. Why should he stay?

He closed the window but still stood looking out. The tract would be silent and white, with a tracery of tracks on the snow, and the marks of disaster covered over. His vision turned inward, encompassing the stream and the tract and the great web of life that informed them both, an entity that had been in balance but whose balance was now being nibbled away like so much of the world's beyond its borders. The creatures which would make the tracks were living the lives for which nature had designed them and knew what they were doing; it was only man, insanely using the intelligence of which he was so proud to frustrate nature, which sought

202

to sustain him, who seemed determined to lose his way and defeat nature and himself.

He turned away from the window, went downstairs, and plugged in the percolator that Mrs. McIntyre had prepared the night before. He did this mechanically, for the mental picture of the tract was still with him. As he stared unseeing at the percolator a rattle at the door brought him back to the room with a start, and he realized that the mailman had dropped the morning mail through the slot in the front door. He went to get it, found a letter from Goodenow, opened it, and read.

The man from the oil company had been in, Goodenow wrote. The company had quietly managed to collect many rights-of-way on each side of them, leaving them almost until last in a sort of squeeze play, and the route of the pipeline was practically set; it would be just about impossible to fight them off now. "I told him we'd go to court," Goodenow went on, "whereupon he smiled at me slightly, as the lions must have smiled at the Christians in the Roman arena, and advised against it. I'm afraid he's right. Vœ victis!" Goodenow hadn't forgotten his classical education, and in his distress had gone back to those happier days.

As they all would if they could, Ohlmstead thought, holding the letter as he walked back to the breakfast room. If they could only go back! He realized he was still holding Goodenow's letter and half raised his hand to look at it, the bearer of the latest but perhaps not the final blow, and the rage that had held him for a time sprang to life again within him. His hand clenched on the letter and crumpled it, and he threw it on the floor.

He stood for a long moment with his eyes closed, and it was all there: the needless road (put in because somebody wanted to sell lots) and what would follow it, the spraying that was uncalled for, the irresponsible power struggle that had let the dam go out, the equally irresponsible failure to seal the old mine that had brought acid drainage down on them, the Seneca and its sewage half controlled by inadequate laws, and the pipeline—all brought about by people who cared about nothing but the dollar or themselves.

He swayed a little, shaken by the intensity of the rising tide of rage, and then got hold of himself; he had been that way before, and it had got him nowhere. He opened his eyes and a sort of calm descended upon him; his legs felt weak, and he sat down. So, then, they had been defeated, and none of the things that had brought about the defeat had been of their own making; these things had fallen upon them, as they were falling in an even more baleful degree on other places elsewhere in the world. He had done what he could, but his best effort seemed to have been the hiding of two peoples' clothes.

It wasn't good enough, it was too parochial and limited, a small, doomed delaying action by a few men on a front that extended far beyond them; and as he faced this conclusion Ohlmstead reached back to the half-formed thought—that he should have done something before, beyond the narrow confines of the tract—that he had pushed into the back of his mind when he was talking to Borrow in front of Borrow's house, and found it half formed no longer.

It told him that it was time he moved out of the little enclave which had preoccupied him into the larger battle, the great struggle not for two thousand acres but for the world. He had heard of, and in his preoccupation ignored, the great rising tide of revolt that brought together militant conservation groups, foundations, dedicated men, and many young people who recognized that the abused earth had been abused enough and more than enough; it was not a limitless resource, the limits were being reached, and they were on the march to save it.

Why had he thought he would go sit uselessly in the sun? He would join them, and the more militant the organization that would take him in, the better.